Thus Saith the Lord

TAMARA DREIER

WestBow
PRESS
A DIVISION OF THOMAS NELSON

WestBow Press books may be ordered through booksellers or by contacting:

WestBow Press
A Division of Thomas Nelson
1663 Liberty Drive
Bloomington, IN 47403
www.westbowpress.com
1-(866) 928-1240

Because of the dynamic nature of the Internet, any web addresses or links contained in this book may have changed since publication and may no longer be valid. The views expressed in this work are solely those of the author and do not necessarily reflect the views of the publisher, and the publisher hereby disclaims any responsibility for them.

Any people depicted in stock imagery provided by Thinkstock are models, and such images are being used for illustrative purposes only.

Certain stock imagery © Thinkstock.

ISBN: 978-1-4497-3133-5 (hc)
ISBN: 978-1-4497-3134-2 (sc)
ISBN: 978-1-4497-3132-8 (e)

Library of Congress Control Number: 2011960360

Printed in the United States of America

WestBow Press rev. date: 11/16/2011

Introduction by Author

I believe God's Holy Word, the Bible, came by inspiration through His Holy Spirit. I believe that God's Holy Spirit, through our confession, will indwell us, cleanse us of all unrighteousness, remove our sins and give us a clean conscience.

God is alive and ever present today speaking to us in His still, quiet voice. We can know His voice and experience an intimate personal relationship with Him, as we open our hearts and invite Him in. The Lord said, "My sheep hear My voice, and I know them, and they follow Me." John 10:27.

Often, we draw near to the Lord in troublesome times. I have found that to be true in my life and it was during my difficult times that I have been the closest to God. Now, I can praise God for all of the trials and tribulations that I have gone through, when I reflect on my past and see how His hand was upon me. Fifteen years ago, I was ministered to through the book, God Calling; because of that book my desire to know Him increased. I wanted to hear what God was saying. I began journaling in the form of a letter to God. I was hurting and desperately seeking God and His healing for my life. At first, I got little solutions to specific problems and answers to questions. I knew I could not think of these answers on my own. God, in His infinite wisdom gave me answers and solutions to my problems. God's Holy Spirit brought scriptures and verses to my memory when I needed them.

My letters to God continued, and I began to write down what He said to me. I knew that I was not the only person in the world who was struggling, lonely, and experiencing difficult times. I prayed for all the other people in the world who were going through the same things; then I would ask God, "What would you say to your people?" Thus, the words I received and share in this book are not only for me, but they are for you too.

His comforting words, spoken over and over to me, have penetrated my heart and spirit. The Lord has healed me and encouraged me. My life has been changed and I know that He lives. He lives inside of me. The words in this book are not my words; they are the Lord's words. He has chosen me to share them with you. I pray God's words would bless you and encourage you as you read and meditate on them.

Tamara Dreier

JANUARY

Therefore, whatever you want men to do to you,
do also to them, for this is the Law and Prophets.

Matthew 7:12

January 1

Thus saith the Lord;

"Make each day a new beginning. Mark your past failures as learning experiences and grow from them. Think of yourself as a little wiser than the day before. Live each day with expectation. Make others your priority instead of yourself. Do unto others as you would have them do unto you. Live each day like there is no tomorrow. Be kind and loving and forgiving to all. When you can do all of these things, you will be just like Me."

January 2

Thus saith the Lord;

"The wintertime is a cold and dry season. People must adapt to this season by taking extra measures to stay warm, safe, and healthy. A person's spiritual life can also change like seasons. When your spiritual life is like winter, stay full of My Word, warm in My love, and healthy in prayer."

January 3

Thus saith the Lord;

"Those who love shall be loved. Those who help shall be helped. Those who give shall receive. Those who shall be a friend will find a friend. Those who are honest shall find the truth. Those who respect shall be respected. Those who are kind shall find kindness. All these things that you give to another you shall receive back. This is a spiritual truth. Practice these things and you will be My peace keepers."

January 4

Thus saith the Lord;

"Do not give up hope; do not cease to pray, for I hear your prayers. All things are possible to him who believes. My power is limitless."

January 5

Thus saith the Lord;

"Oh, My precious child, you think that you do not do enough for Me. The day will come when you will see all that you have done for Me, for nothing goes unnoticed by Me. Your prayers bless Me. Your praises bring Me much pleasure."

January 6

Thus saith the Lord;

"My precious child, I hear your prayers. I know your cares and concerns even before you ask. It is good that you bring these to Me, for you are right; I am in control. I can change all things. Trust in Me, for I will do what is best for you and your concerns. Nothing is impossible or too hard for Me. Do not judge the sins of others. Lift them to Me, and I will be the judge of them. My blessings are upon you and you shall feel them and see them. Rejoice, for I am in control."

January 7

Thus saith the Lord;

"Delight thyself also in Me and I will give thee the desires of thine heart."

January 8

Thus saith the Lord;

"There is a time and a season for all things: a time to sow, a time to reap, a time for sorrow, a time to rejoice, a time for work, and a time for rest. Just as the seasons change, so do your circumstances change. Do not worry about tomorrow, for I only give you what you need for today. Just as sure as the snow will melt and the spring will come, so will solutions come and your prayers will be answered. Be confident and know that I love you and am taking care of you. The *Son* will surely shine."

January 9

Thus saith the Lord;

"If My people will humble themselves before Me and pray and turn from their wicked ways, I will forgive them of their sins and heal their land, their homes, and their families, and I will be their God and they will be My children. They will find peace, love, joy, health, and prosperity. They will run and not grow weary. They will have peace during the storms of life. They will not lack any good thing. They will not be dry. Fear will be far from them. They shall ask anything according to My will and it shall be given to them, all of this and more, because I love them."

January 10

Thus saith the Lord;

"You must be born again to enter into My kingdom. Call upon Me and confess Me as your Lord and Savior. Acknowledge your sins and ask for My forgiveness. I will wash you as white as snow and birth a new heart in you. My Spirit will begin to renew you and you will be a new creation in Christ."

January 11

Thus saith the Lord;

"I have come that you would have life—life abundantly. You must learn to live in this abundant life. It is a gift from Me, freely given to all that seek and ask. Strive for it so that your yoke will be light and so that your joy may be full. Allow Me to be in control. Let Me guide. Be submissive to Me and My leading. Do not let the cares of the world weigh you down. Lift them up to Me, for I care for you. I love you and I will not leave you alone."

January 12

Thus saith the Lord;

"I desire that you be close to Me. I desire that you be happy and content. I desire that you spend time with Me. So give. Give until you receive joy. *Worship!* Worship until your joy overflows. Spend time with Me—until your heart is content. Then I will have My wish for you."

January 13

Thus saith the Lord;

"No, you are not your own; you have been bought with a price. Die to yourself, for you no longer live, but it is I who lives in you. When you realize that it is I who lives in you and not you who live, you will be able to have self-control over all the areas that you now struggle with. Remember, not your will but My will be done. Live for self and the rewards are temporal. Live for Me and the rewards are eternal. Die to yourself and the struggles in your mind will eventually banish. I died that you might have life more abundantly. Now, you die to your selfish needs and desires that I might live through you."

January 14

Thus saith the Lord;

"Love is a priceless gift. It cannot be purchased with any amount of money. Love is more than a feeling; it is a choice. You must choose to love. You must choose to be loved. My love is given freely to all. Will you choose to let Me love you? Love is the greatest gift of all. Love will cover a multitude of sins. Love endures forever. Love is patient. Love is kind. I am love. Accept My love this day and My love will flow through you and give you new life, like the life giving blood flowing through your veins."

January 15

Thus saith the Lord;

"My strength is made perfect in your weakness. When you are weak, I am strong. Let Me help you with everything, My child. I am willing, and I am able. Give Me all that besets your mind—no more hassles, no more worries, for now they are mine. Happy you will be, to trust in Me, knowing that I am able to help thee. When you are happy, you can do more work for Me. I will be blessed."

January 16

Thus saith the Lord;

"I love you so much, My child. There is nothing that I would not do for you. My love endures forever. Let My love dwell richly in your heart and mind. For when you know and feel My love, your life will change. Happy you will be to let the love of God set you free. Love is the key to many of My treasures. Love is the key to happiness. Love is the key to contentment. Love is the key to forgiveness. Love is the key to success. Take My love this day and use all that you need and pass the rest on."

January 17

Thus saith the Lord;

"I have made the mighty rivers to flow and not to run dry. I have allowed My Holy Spirit to flow into your life, and it is up to you not to let it run dry—to keep it flowing. You must give away what I have given you before a new supply will come to you. For example, if I give to you joy then let that joy freely flow into someone else's life. If I give you peace, then help someone else find that peace. If I give you love, then pour it out onto someone else. This is My divine law of giving. Give and it will be given back to you."

January 18

Thus saith the Lord;

"What seems to be bad or unpleasant to you in your life is not always so, because your eyes are of this world. You cannot see the accomplishments being made on the inside. Things are not always as they may seem. Do not try to decipher what I am doing. Continue in My Word and in prayer with Me even when you do not feel like it. My work will continue whether you feel like it or not. As long as you walk with Me, My work will continue in your life also—even when you do not feel as though it is, or want it to. The experiences are not always pleasant, but the outcome is rewarding. I love you, and I will help you."

January 19

Thus saith the Lord;

"It is good when you allow Me to work out the solutions to your problems. Give Me control over every situation, for I know what is best. If there is something that you need to do in the situation, it will be revealed to you. Do not fret or worry. Do not be sad. I can make something that appears to be bad to the natural man and can turn it into something good and wonderful for the kingdom of God. Learn to live in peace and joy. Know that I am in control. Believe and trust in Me for I made you, I love you, and I will take care of you. Will you let Me? Give all to Me."

January 20

Thus saith the Lord;

"You cannot do anything without Me. You must wait on Me. Wait—until I give you the answer, direct your path, spur you on, and lead your way. Do nothing out of anger, for this is not from Me. The tongue is an unruly evil and when used in anger can destroy everything that I have been working on. Resist anger and it will flee from you. Pursue peace and love. Pray for those who make you angry."

January 21

Thus saith the Lord;

"Seek Me first and My kingdom and all things will be added to you. I am a rewarder of those who diligently seek Me. I give the desires of their heart to those who delight in Me. I am patient and kind. I am a friend that sticks closer than a brother. I am always there. I will never leave you nor forsake you. Give your burdens and cares to Me. I know what you need better than you know yourself. I will guide and direct you in the way you are to go. You belong to Me and I love you. Trust in Me. Rest in Me."

January 22

Thus saith the Lord;

"Live each day with Me. Spend time with Me. You will grow more and more like Me. The world would be changed if more people prayed like you. Prayer changes things. Prayer changes people. Prayer changes circumstances. Prayer wards off evil. Prayer is not only communion with Me, but it also sets into motion those things that are spoken."

January 23

Thus saith the Lord;

"Give all to Me. I will continue the good work that I have begun until the end. I am at work. Everything I do is good. Even the bad—I can turn into good. Let not your heart be troubled. You shall hear of My work, and you will see answers to your prayers. You will see results."

January 24

Thus saith the Lord;

"My ways are not your ways. My thoughts are not your thoughts. I see all. I hear all. I know all. I know the beginning to the end. Just as you think you know what is best for your children because you are older and wiser: I also know what is best for My children. I allow mistakes to be made, sometimes over and over again. I am a loving God. This does not mean I will not allow for one to hurt from his mistakes. Some lessons are learned quickly and painlessly. Other lessons are harder to learn. Are you not thankful that I have not given up on you for not learning a lesson quickly? Do not give up on people. I look for the possibilities and potential in all. Everyone is unique and everyone has something good in them and about them. Find it."

January 25

Thus saith the Lord;

"You are wise, My child, to seek Me as your counsel. I am the Almighty Counselor. I am a help in time of trouble. I will help you; I will answer you. Continue to look to Me for all your needs. I am always available. I am working on your behalf. If I am for you, who can be against you? Nothing is too hard for Me. Do not be sad nor let your heart be troubled. Have I not worked out all your other problems? You have seen My hand at work in the past. I am a very present help in the time of trouble. Trust Me."

January 26

Thus saith the Lord;

"Learn to live in My presence, for you will be in My presence for eternity. Remember that every tangible thing in this world is temporal and shall pass away, but My Words shall last forever. The closer you get to Me and the more time you spend with Me, the less the things in the world will trouble you. Invest time in others that they may also see eternity, for if every child of mine saved one lost soul, the whole world would be saved."

January 27

Thus saith the Lord;

"I shall take care of you. Abide in Me and I will abide in you. I will lead you into the land of plenty. I will make the sun to shine in your hearts even on the dreary days. No harm shall come to you. My gentle leading will guide your way. You will not veer from My path. No one, by any means, can change the plans that I have for you. Place your loved ones in My care, and I will do the same for them too. You see, My Father has given you to Me, and no one can snatch you from Me. The same is true when you give your loved ones to Me—no one can snatch them from Me. Be confident. Be trusting. No worries, no cares, because you have entrusted them to Me. I love you."

January 28

Thus saith the Lord;

"I am a jealous God. If anyone puts anything before Me, I am jealous. I feel your pain. You have suffered much, My child. I came that you might have life and a more abundant life. Do not fear, for low I am with you even to the end of the earth. I guide your steps. I have plans for you. Know that I love you and will never leave you nor forsake you. I forgive you and remember your sins no more. Live each day with Me and I shall sustain you. I will meet your every need, for I am the Lord your God and you are My child."

January 29

Thus saith the Lord;

"Do not be sad, for I have the power to turn what appears to be a bad situation into something beautiful and good. Do not see things the way the world sees things. Look up and rejoice, for I am in control."

January 30

Thus saith the Lord;

"I have always been at work and am working even as we speak. Be patient and know that I am in control. You will rejoice and be exceedingly glad."

January 31

Thus saith the Lord;

"Faith is: believing that you have received something before it has manifested. To all, I have given a measure of faith. Faith comes by hearing and hearing by the Word of God, for without faith it is impossible to please Me. Faith can be increased and grow. Pray that you would have more faith. Through My Holy Spirit you have been given power to do all the works that I did and greater works than I did, because I have gone to be with My Father. Hope is not faith, but these three go together: hope, faith, and trust. Ask anything in My name, according to My Word, and you shall receive it. When you ask for it, believe that you have received it already."

FEBRUARY

My sheep hear My voice, and I know them,
and they follow Me.

John 10:27

February 1

Thus saith the Lord;

"My child, listening is an important part of your relationship with Me. I desire to commune with you. Take time to listen often, each day, many times. It is vital that you hear My instructions. You will know My voice. My sheep know My voice and do not heed to another. My glorious plans are unfolding for your life. Have no fear about your future, for I am in control. I love these times that we spend together. My love surrounds you. Feel My love. Feel My touch. You desire to spend time with those whom you love. I love you and I want to spend time with you."

February 2

Thus saith the Lord;

"You are My shining light to many people, some of whom you would not even believe. Many lives have been touched by you. All that you need—I can provide. All that you ask—shall come to pass."

February 3

Thus saith the Lord;

"Peace be to you. Be still and know that I am God. When you trust Me totally: you will be happy, you will be content, and you will be worry-free. I am able and willing, but you do not let Me do the work that you have asked Me to do. Step back and rest and let Me accomplish all that you have asked Me to do. I will tell you the things that I need you to do for Me. You must also be willing and able and My plans will unfold."

February 4

Thus saith the Lord;

"Do not worry or fret, My child, for I am in control. All things are at My disposal. I will reveal them and give them to you at the appropriate time. Continue to trust Me. Trust Me more. Love Me more. Focus on Me. Give Me all of your attention, for I am doing a mighty thing. You will be exceedingly happy. I have the keys to your future, and they are bright and prosperous. Try to be consistently happy because nothing, and I mean nothing, can change the plans that I have for you. You are blessed."

February 5

Thus saith the Lord;

"Every situation has a negative and a positive way to look at it. For example, when a relationship goes sour and you split up, you can view it as the end of a good thing, or it can be viewed as the beginning of a new thing. A day that the sun is shining half of the day can be viewed as partly cloudy or partly sunny. A glass of water to the half-way mark can be viewed as half-empty or half-full. Choose to be positive and your outlook on your everyday situations will change."

February 6

Thus saith the Lord;

"To each person I have a calling, a plan, and a purpose. Each one is different and unique and no two people are alike. I need each person to accomplish My will and My plans for the world. They are all linked together in perfect harmony in the same fashion that the human body operates."

February 7

Thus saith the Lord;

"Learn to sing as the birds sing without care or worry. Singing, to the natural man, is done because one is happy. But I say to you, sing when you are unhappy and it will make you happy. Praise Me in song, for I love your praises. The enemy will flee for he hates your praises. Joy will rise up in your spirit and I will be blessed, for it will be a sweet, sweet sound in My ear."

February 8

Thus saith the Lord;

"This day nothing will come your way that I cannot handle: not the smallest care or the biggest problem. I have an answer and solution for all. Talk to Me like I am your confidant. Ask Me what I would do in your situation. Just as a child confides in a parent, confide also in Me. Let not your heart be troubled or afraid. Let My love flow freely."

February 9

Thus saith the Lord;

"You are My shining light. How you do shine forth to many. Do not fear, for all your blessings come from My hand, and they are many. You shall always have what you need. Let your needs be made known to Me. Do not fear what the future holds. For I know all, I see all, and I have plans for you. Seek My plans."

February 10

Thus saith the Lord;

"Disobedience is as witchcraft. Pray against the spirit of witchcraft. Pray against any curses passed down from generation to generation. They can be blotted out by the blood of *Jesus,* because I hung on the cross as a curse. I died for your sins that they may be forgiven: by My blood you will have new life—a better life for you. My blood is life giving, My blood is cleansing, My blood is healing, My blood is protection. It has already been shed for you and your loved ones. Claim it and live under it, for it belongs to you—the blood covenant of your Lord and Savior."

February 11

Thus saith the Lord;

"My children will suffer many things; most will be caused by their own neglect or disobedience. I have promised to never leave them nor forsake them. When they call upon Me, I will help them. Suffering is not always bad, but it is a way to change, learn, and grow. Often times it is through one's suffering that they come to know Me. Welcome changes, which often come with suffering."

February 12

Thus saith the Lord;

"Abide in Me and I will abide in you. Call My name and I will be there. Say *'Jesus'* and demons will flee. Say *'Jesus'* and you will feel My peace. Keep your eyes on Me and not on the storms around you. I will keep you in perfect peace and will not let you fall. I shall give you My strength and uphold you. Your house will be built upon the rock and it cannot be torn down. I give My angels charge over you. Continue to learn, love, and laugh."

February 13

Thus saith the Lord;

"Trust Me with your whole heart and lean not to your own understanding. You cannot perceive how I may supply your needs, answer your requests, or work out certain situations. My ways are higher than your ways and My thoughts are higher than your thoughts. Do not limit My powers, because I know what is best for you. My way is the best way. Give Me your problems, cares, and concerns. Ask of Me everything big and small. I will show you, guide you, and answer you at the appropriate time in the best way possible. It will bring honor and glory to My name and you will rejoice and be exceedingly glad."

February 14

Thus saith the Lord;

"All that you ask for, I can do. My power is limitless and My time is never ending. As far as the east is from the west is how great My love is for you. Your sins are forgiven. Do not dwell on your imperfections. I see the possibilities and the good in you. You are righteous in My eyes. You have been made heirs of My kingdom. I say to you that it is good to bear one another's burdens; then lift them to Me, for I will make your load light and I will give you peace."

February 15

Thus saith the Lord;

"My hands never cease to work. I never grow tired and do not sleep. There is so much to do in My kingdom. No prayer goes unanswered. I need laborers to help with My work. Without your prayers My work cannot continue. It is you who release My power into people's lives and situations. I need you. The course of the world could be changed by your prayers. Continue to pray about all things. You are My faithful child in whom I am well-pleased."

February 16

Thus saith the Lord;

"I never said your life with Me would be easy. I said that I would never leave you nor forsake you; that I would go before you; prepare your way, and that I would help you, lead you, and guide you. You must learn to live in Me, and let Me live in you."

February 17

Thus saith the Lord;

"Say in all situations, 'Lord, not my will but your will be done.' Don't try to decide how to handle them but let Me have My way. I will help you. You could be stress-free in your life and full of joy and peace because you have the All Mighty, the All Knowing, the Master, the Maker of all to guide you in every decision you need to make, and He will work out all the solutions to your problems. You will add quality to your life, and less time will be wasted worrying over nothing. Ultimately you will only be doing things once—the right way—My way."

February 18

Thus saith the Lord;

"My blessings are upon you and all that you ask for you shall receive. My hand is upon you. Financial blessings will be yours. Trust in Me with your whole heart and lean not to your own understanding. Continue to pray. Dwell on Me and the good things to come."

February 19

Thus saith the Lord;

"Oh, My precious child, how your light does shine forth. Your prayers do not go unanswered. Wonders are unfolding. Just as no man can stop the day from turning into night, no one can stop My will and My work in you. Each day is a new beginning. You are becoming more like Me. Let My Words dwell richly in your heart."

February 20

Thus saith the Lord;

"I have much more for you to do. I have much more in store for you. All I have ever wanted was willing hearts: hearts to serve, hearts to love, hearts to give, care, and be used by Me. I need that. I love that. You will abound in blessings. You shall see. You shall see answers to your prayers. You shall see the fruits of your rewards. I am taking you into a new level of joy. Let your joy be full."

February 21

Thus saith the Lord;

"Each child of mine is special in his own way. For you are wondrously made. You are unique and there is none like you. You are My child and I am your God. Fear not change, for changes must come, but I never change. I am the same yesterday, today, and forever. Expect a miracle. I am the God of miracles."

February 22

Thus saith the Lord;

"Others may seem to let you down. Others may seem to disappoint you. I will never do that to you. Look to Me for everything, because I am always here. I never change and My Words will endure forever. Seek My ways and My Words. They will comfort you. They are life changing and life giving. All that have them will abide satisfied."

February 23

Thus saith the Lord;

"I help those who want My help and ask for My help. I am always willing and ready, but many will not allow Me to help them. Pray for those in need, because if they do not ask for My help, you can intercede on their behalf."

February 24

Thus saith the Lord;

"This is the day that I have made—rejoice and be glad in it. Give to Me your first fruits, and then I will multiply plenty for you. Give Me the first part of your day, and then you will have plenty left for your other responsibilities and they will be blessed. Give to Me the first tithe of your finances and the rest will be blessed by Me. Do not think that you do not have enough for yourself so that you cannot give to Me. Give to Me first and I will multiply what is left for yourself. My blessings will abound."

February 25

Thus saith the Lord;

"Do not dwell on your own problems. There are many other people who are less fortunate than you. Pray for them. Try to lessen their burdens. By helping others, your problems will not seem so bad, for they are not as bad as you perceive them to be. By lifting your burdens to Me you will feel lighter and better able to help carry another person's burdens. You will make them feel better and I will make you feel better. I love you and care for you."

February 26

Thus saith the Lord;

"I am a rewarder of those who diligently seek Me. I am doing many, mighty works in your life and for others around you. Most of My work cannot be seen by the natural eye, for much of My work is done from the inside out. You cannot see what is in the heart. It is even hard for you to know your own heart. Be content with what you have, for you lack nothing. My angels protect and watch over you. I love you."

February 27

Thus saith the Lord;

"There will be a great financial blessing coming your way. I understand your needs and your desires. You do have a giving heart and you will bless many financially and spiritually. You have My gift of peace. Pass it on. The more you give, the more you will receive; this is true in all things. Remember this, it is My divine law."

February 28

Thus saith the Lord;

"My power is as Niagara Falls. Nothing, and I mean nothing, can stop it. It shall come in like a flood and the enemy shall be destroyed. The same way that a fire sweeps through a house destroying everything in its path; that is how My Spirit shall be in your life, destroying the works of the enemy. My Spirit conquers, My Spirit restores, My Spirit is life, and he who has it shall abide satisfied. When the going gets rough, do not give up, for you are on the brink of a miracle. Lo, I am with you, I hear your cries, I feel your pain, and I will heal you. Take comfort and be filled with My peace. I love you."

MARCH

My son, give attention to My Words; Incline your
ear to My sayings. Do not let them depart from
your eyes; Keep them in the midst of your heart;
For they are life to those who find them, and
health to all their flesh.

Proverbs 4: 20-22

March 1

Thus saith the Lord;

"Try to be happy. Know that I am in control, and I will take care of you. Do not let circumstances around you alter your joy that I have given to you. These circumstances can in no way alter My plans for you. Just as the dandelions outside are many, so are My blessings for you. A flowerbed has many beautiful flowers, growing and nurtured by the good soil and rain. If the weeds are not continually plucked out, they will overtake and eventually kill the flowers. You are My beautiful flower that I am trying to nurture and grow. You must continually root out the weeds in your life by My Word. My Words are life and health to your bones. My Words do not return unto Me void."

March 2

Thus saith the Lord;

"Know that confusion is not of Me. I am leading you in your life and I am in control. I have very definite plans for your life—plans to prosper you and bless you. I shall never leave you nor forsake you. Do not fear. All things will work out for My glory."

March 3

Thus saith the Lord;

"Worry or fret not, for this accomplishes nothing. It is a waste of your time. I have told you many times that I am in control. Do you not see My hand constantly at work in your life? Spend more time in My Word and talking to Me, and less time will be wasted."

March 4

Thus saith the Lord;

"You must become as a little child. A little child is so trusting. I will not hurt you, but only love you. I will never leave you; I am right by your side. I never make a promise that I cannot keep. I only tell you the truth. I will care for you and provide for you. I will keep you in My arms of love. It was through many of life's experiences and countless hurts and pains from others that you have learned not to trust. I can heal those hurts and pains. I have come to heal the broken-hearted and bind up their wounds. As you draw closer to Me and know Me better, you will be able to trust Me more. For I have said, trust Me with your whole heart and lean not to your own understanding. When you can do this, it will be because you have given Me total control of your life—happy will you be."

March 5

Thus saith the Lord;

"Follow Me and I will make you fishers of men. All are seeking to serve someone. You are only to point the way. Unleash My power through prayer to lead the way. Be a living example of My life. Spend time with Me. Commune with Me and I will commune with you. Be useable, be teachable, be reachable, and you will be in My will."

March 6

Thus saith the Lord;

"I am everywhere that you go. You need not look too hard and you will see Me: everything lovely, everything beautiful—I am there, a constant reminder of your Lord and Maker. Think of Me often. Talk to Me throughout the day. You will feel My presence, and My help will make your day a little easier. You are not alone."

March 7

Thus saith the Lord;

"No man can tell the day, the time, or the hour in which I will return. Be ever watching and ever ready. Do not put off until tomorrow what you can do today. Be ye perfect as I am perfect. Love, laugh, and live each day as though it were your last, for you do not know what tomorrow holds."

March 8

Thus saith the Lord;

"You must be in My Word to learn and grow. Commune with Me more, and spend more time with me. Food is an essential to live and grow; so is My Word essential to live and grow spiritually. Learn and live by My Word. You take in the Word and I bless it and make you grow—just like eating real food. All you have to do is eat; the food and your body will do the rest. Take in My Word and I do the rest."

March 9

Thus saith the Lord;

"Be joyful, My child, for you are on the brink of a miracle. Your prayers do not go unanswered."

March 10

Thus saith the Lord;

"My rain cometh; it comes to all those who are thirsty; My rain cometh. You shall drink and be satisfied, for I am the well of life. To all of those whom I have chosen, My reign cometh. You shall reign together with Me, throughout all eternity. There will be no more sorrow and no more pain. How glorious the day, when we will at last all be together. Each new day, we are one day closer. Until then, drink of My Spirit and be filled with My Spirit. I am your God and you are My child. Bow your head and be blessed."

March 11

Thus saith the Lord;

"You cannot control people: you can only guide them, teach them, and love them. I send you to help point the way. You are My eyes, ears, mouth, and loving touch. Do not give up on the lost, for they need much guidance."

March 12

Thus saith the Lord;

"You are My shining light. You will shine My light into many lives, and your prayers will not go unanswered. My supply will never end. My blessings surround you. I give My angels charge over you and all yours."

March 13

Thus saith the Lord;

"I am blessing you with every spiritual blessing. I am providing for your every need. Look for the good in all. Look to help others. I will send many across your path and you will touch many lives. Remember you are the light of the world and many will be attracted to you."

March 14

Thus saith the Lord;

"Do not worry about anything, for worrying accomplishes nothing. Seek Me and My kingdom and all things will be added to you. Be filled with My joy knowing that I am in control and that I love you and will take care of you."

March 15

Thus saith the Lord;

"Help others—try to make another person's day a little nicer—be kind. Make someone smile or laugh, for what you give away will come back to you. Try to brighten someone else's day. Be more concerned for another's welfare rather than your own. Give—give—give. Give of yourself. Give of your time. Be less concerned about yourself. Put others first."

March 16

Thus saith the Lord;

"I will touch My people. They will run and not get weary. They shall mount on the wings of eagles and they shall fly. My people shall hear My voice. My people shall obey Me. I shall turn their sadness into joy. I will fill their cups to overflowing. They shall not lack any good thing. I will lift them up out of the miry clay. They shall be the head and not the tail. I will teach them My Words and My ways. They shall prosper."

March 17

Thus saith the Lord;

"I say to you, that you will see many changes. Many things will come to pass. You are a blessing to others and you will be blessed. Be full of joy for you have much to be joyful for."

March 18

Thus saith the Lord;

"I see all. I feel all. I know all. I made all. Do not worry, My precious child. It is very soon and you will begin to see changes in many areas of your life."

March 19

Thus saith the Lord;

"I have unending love for you. My love covers a multitude of sins. My love is kind and patient. I am here. I am here to wipe away your tears. Do not be sad, but rejoice because I am in control. You are in the palm of My hand. No evil thing can touch you. I have many wonderful things to give you. You are so blessed. There should be no room for sadness."

March 20

Thus saith the Lord;

"Obtain wisdom. Wisdom produces wealth. Knowledge can be gained from Me in My Word. Read My Word. The more you read, the more you know. The more you know, the more you will grow. Faith will be increased. Faith comes by hearing and hearing by the Word of God. The more you grow like Me, the wiser you will become. My ways are simple—even a child can understand My ways, but they are hidden to the wise of the world. My Words do not return to Me void. Confess My Words. They are life to your flesh and health to your bones. Learn and live. Be blessed."

March 21

Thus saith the Lord;

"I will give you things to do for Me. Lift your cares and the concerns of others, up in prayer. Without your prayers, I can do nothing. You shall be My prayer warrior. This is what I will have you do for Me. I will not reveal everything to you so you will not worry or be sad. Give all your cares and concerns to Me. Your calling is mighty and much can be accomplished through prayer, including changing world affairs. You don't have to leave home. I will teach you more and more how to use the power in prayer. There is much power in prayer."

March 22

Thus saith the Lord;

"Just as the rains and storms of this world come, you know they are only for a period of time. Some storms are short; some are longer, but eventually they come to an end. So are the storms in your life; they are temporal and only endure for a period of time. Both kinds of storms are meaningful and have a purpose. Know that the storms in your life are part of My plan; by knowing this, you will benefit greatly. You will grow. You will rejoice. Rains and storms are revitalization to the life and the land; so are the ones in your lives to your soul and spirit. See this and welcome this."

March 23

Thus saith the Lord;

"You are My beloved child, in whom I am well pleased. You ask much of Me and it is My great pleasure to give to you all that you ask for. Continue to seek Me, ask what you will and I will do it for you. I am a rewarder of those who diligently seek Me. I love those that love Me. Your love for Me is great. Blessings are coming, not because you deserve them, but because I am a blesser."

March 24

Thus saith the Lord;

"My eyes are upon you and all that you do. Some things are pleasing and some displeasing. Ask Me to cleanse you daily of all unrighteousness. I will make you pure. I am changing you, molding and making you more into My image. I am a forgiving God and I remember no more. The past is forgotten and you should not dwell on your past failures and sins. I can turn what seems bad into something good and wonderful. You are learning. You are growing. Love all those whom I bring across your path. Love the sinner, but not the sin. Nothing will turn My love away from you. I love you at all times, everywhere, every day, every way. Remember that."

March 25

Thus saith the Lord;

"Oh, My precious child, do not fret about your life. Do you not know that I am in control! I formed the world and the universe in six days. Nothing is too hard for Me. Things you ask of Me are little. They are like pebbles in My hands. Know I care for you and love you. I am guiding you by My eye. I shall keep you under My wings. I have a very definite plan for your life: plans to prosper you and plans to use you. Continue to pray about all things. You will see the answers. For none of your prayers go unanswered. The answer may not always be as you think it should be, but My way is the best way. You must trust Me. You say you trust Me, but you must trust Me more. You say you believe My Word, but you must believe Me more. You say you love Me, but you must love Me more. Push out all doubt, fear, worry, and anxiety. All these things will rob you of trust, belief, and love of Me. **Pray, pray, pray!** You cannot pray enough. The world would be changed if more people would pray."

March 26

Thus saith the Lord;

"You are My beloved child, in whom I am well pleased. Your faith shall be rewarded. Believe that what you have asked for you have received. This is the faith that I would have you walk in. Faith is: believing that you have received it before it has manifested. The enemy has come to kill, steal, and destroy. I am the avenger of the enemy. Put on the whole armor of God. Fight the good fight of faith and stand strong. *Let me fight your battles!* Use My Word as a weapon. Do not let the enemy steal your joy. Remember all the things I have told you, for you are a threat to his kingdom. Greater is He that is in you than he that is in the world. I have equipped you with all that you need to conquer. You are a conqueror. Know that I love you and that I am with you even to the end of the world. I bless you. Now receive it."

March 27

Thus saith the Lord;

"Do not do anything drastically. But through prayer and supplication, let your requests be made known unto Me. Do not respond in anger, but only by seeking Me, so you can respond in love. Often times, My plans get altered by My children responding drastically of their own free will. Do not seek to change the course of the world by yourselves, because it is only I who can make the changes. You need to allow Me to do all things. Let Me accomplish the work. Love all whom I bring across your path, no matter what state they are in. Do not judge, for by what measure you judge, you shall be judged. My child, you need more joy. Lift your burdens to Me, and I shall carry them for you."

March 28

Thus saith the Lord;

"Faith brings Me much pleasure; without faith you cannot please Me. Your faith will be increased. Faith comes by hearing, and hearing by the Word of God. Faith is an essential key in prayer. Your prayers are mighty in My kingdom. Your prayers shall not go unanswered. Continue to seek Me and My kingdom, and all things shall be added to you. Many blessings shall come your way and you shall be a blessing to many. Do not grow weary in well-doing, for in due time you shall reap. Continue to knock and doors will be opened. Seek and you shall find and I will teach you many things. You shall begin a spiritual level that you have not known before. Ask and it shall be given to you. Let your joy be full, for you have much to be joyful for."

March 29

Thus saith the Lord;

"Let Me handle it. Let Me handle your cares, your concerns, your finances, your worries, your problems. I can help you with everything in your life. Lift them all to Me, for I care for you."

March 30

Thus saith the Lord;

"My power is limitless. My giving is endless. My love never ceases. All belongs to Me. All is for Me to give. I want you to have all that I have. Learn to give freely just as I give all freely. The more you give, the more you will receive. Be a cheerful giver, for I see the hearts. When you give to others you also give to Me."

March 31

Thus saith the Lord;

"Do not be in a hurry. Do not be rushed, for I am not in a hurry. My time is priceless. My time is everlasting. My time is not your time. My Words shall endure forever. My promises are true. I will do all that I have said that I would do. My time is perfect. I do not withhold because you cannot have it, but rather the time is not yet. There is a season and a time for all things. I am in control; I am working in your life; and I am answering your prayers in the best possible way."

APRIL

Finally, My brethren, be strong in the Lord and in the power of His might. Put on the whole armor of God, that you may be able to stand against the wiles of the devil. For we do not wrestle against flesh and blood, but against principalities, against powers, against the rulers of the darkness of this age, against spiritual hosts of wickedness in the heavenly places, Therefore take up the whole armor of God, that you may be able to withstand in the evil day, and having done all, to stand. Stand therefore, having girded your waist with truth, having put on the breastplate of righteousness, and having shod your feet with the preparation of the gospel of peace; above all, taking the shield of faith with which you will be able to quench all the fiery darts of the wicked one.

Ephesians 6:10-16

April 1

Thus saith the Lord;

"Be strong in My strength to battle the enemy, for he has come in might against those who threaten him. Be not afraid, for it is I who fight the battles. When he puts thoughts in your mind, rebuke him and he must flee. Stand on My Word and all that I have told you. You will be blessed."

April 2

Thus saith the Lord;

"Oh, My precious child, you bring Me much joy and I am very pleased with your prayers. Let your requests be made known to Me. I know your needs before you even ask. I will answer each and every prayer. I will guide you by My eye. You will know what you are to do and when to do it. Do not fear, for I go before you and prepare your way. Be patient and wait on Me. I am doing a mighty work in your life. You will be exceedingly glad. Rejoice, even now, rejoice."

April 3

Thus saith the Lord;

"Seek My face and spend time with Me. There will be times of joy and peace. Alone times—just you and me; quiet times—resting in My love; communing one with the other. I have much to say so take time, be quiet, and listen. Listening is as important as praying. If only My people will listen to Me. Listening comes before obedience. For you must first hear and then obey. Learn to be quiet and take time to listen. Commune with Me and I will commune with you. This is what friends do. You are My friend."

April 4

Thus saith the Lord;

"This is the first day of the rest of your life, for all past failures and sins have been forgotten. I remember them no more. All past hurts and pains are healed, for by My stripes you are healed. Each day is a new beginning. You need not live in shame or torment. My grace is sufficient for you. Live in My love. I love you."

April 5

Thus saith the Lord;

"My plans are unfolding before your eyes. You shall see wonders and miracles in answer to your prayers. I came that you might have life more abundantly. You will walk in this abundant life. You shall have much to give to others. You shall receive the gift of giving. Joy will overflow from this giving in your heart and to the hearts of others. When you give to others you also give to Me. You are blessed and many will be blessed by you."

April 6

Thus saith the Lord;

"I will make your light shine brighter—you shall touch many lives. I am sending many across your path—please pray for each one. Do not become burdened by those who cross your path—just pray and lift them to Me. Shine your light—love—they will see Me in you. Your prayers do not go unanswered. You will see many answers to prayers. You will see My hand at work. You will see healings; you will see miracles; you will be blessed, and you are even being blessed each and every day."

April 7

Thus saith the Lord;

"You have a special place in My heart. I am greatly pleased by what you have asked for! Today you shall see My hand at work and I shall bless you. Do not fear what tomorrow may bring. My supply is sufficient for today. It sorrows Me greatly when you are so sorrowful. Find the good things in your life and dwell on them. Think on what is good and wonderful. Banish all thoughts of evil and bad. Be thankful and praise Me and depression will flee. What you have asked for will be given to you."

April 8

Thus saith the Lord;

"Your supply is on the way. Know that I will care for you and provide for you."

Philippians 4:19 "And My God shall supply all your needs according to His riches in glory by Christ *Jesus*."

Prayer: Dear Lord, supply all My needs according to your riches and glory in Heaven in *Jesus'* name, Amen.

April 9

Thus saith the Lord;

"You shall see My hand at work. The day will come when whatever you say shall come to pass. Be careful what you ask for, because what you say will happen. You have the power to bless others and to curse others."

April 10

Thus saith the Lord;

"I have many plans for your life—ways to prosper you—ways to use you. You shall touch many lives. You have touched so many already. You have the power to bless others. You are mighty in My kingdom and you have done great things. You are being blessed in many ways. Continue to reach out to others."

April 11

Thus saith the Lord;

"The more time you spend with Me, the more you will be like Me. The more I will pour out to you and the better you will get to know Me. I shall reveal many mighty things to you."

April 12

Thus saith the Lord;

"Be patient, My child. Do not worry. Trust Me. I will take care of you. Above all things—trust Me."

April 13

Thus saith the Lord;

"Never think that I do not want you, need you, or love you. I stand waiting with open arms. I rejoice in our friendship. I wait for the times that we spend together. I am never too busy. Call upon Me and I will be there. I do not condemn. Any condemnation that you may feel is not from Me. Your judgment of yourself is harsher than mine. Know that you are forgiven."

April 14

Thus saith the Lord;

"You truly are a gift to Me, for My Father has given you to Me. I cherish all those whom My Father gives to Me. He loves Me and I love Him. You were not given to Me like a slave to a master: rather that I may serve and help you. All that has been asked of you is that you love Me and keep My commandments. It is I who shall be your servant. Will you let Me serve you today?"

April 15

Thus saith the Lord;

"I will do all that you ask Me to do. Know that the works of the enemy are being destroyed because of your prayers. Unless you ask, I can do nothing. I need you so that I may accomplish My work on this earth. My will and My ways are being established in your heart. Do not fear, for I have you under the shadow of My wings. Goodness and mercy shall follow you all the days of your life. Don't worry, be happy, and love all whom I bring across your path. When you love one another you also love Me."

April 16

Thus saith the Lord;

"My blessed child, I see the hearts of men, woman, and children. I am moved by your faith, belief, and love in Me. I do hear your prayers. I know your needs. A day will come when you will see how foolish you were wasting so much time fretting and worrying over all the small stuff, when I have you in the palm of My hand. The day is coming when all your needs will be met; all your desires come true; and My blessings will pour out to you like mighty waters—you will rejoice. Your eyes are set on the world more than they are on Me. You need spiritual eyes, spiritual ears, and a spiritual mind. I will send people across your path that is in need. Give to them the things that they need and you shall be blessed."

April 17

Thus saith the Lord;

"Lift your hands to Me and I will bless you. I am teaching you much. Teaching is a process that cannot be done quickly. I am very pleased with your progress. Know that I am your great teacher and there are many little lessons along the way. You do not see them all as lessons, teachings, and growing opportunities. You must begin to see all things like this. Continue to come together in prayer, for two are better than one. I have brought you two together for this purpose. You have been faithful and I shall reward your faithfulness."

April 18

Thus saith the Lord;

"I move people in your life to help you, and I move people out of your life who hinder you. I am in control and you cannot change the plans that I have for your life, as long as you continue to walk with Me. Do not fret or worry. You must know that all is well. I feel your pain—I am sad when you are sad. Do not let others determine your happiness. I am all that you need."

April 19

Thus saith the Lord;

"I am all you need. When you realize this and practice this, you will be content."

April 20

Thus saith the Lord;

"Oh, My precious child, your faith is great. You shall accomplish mighty things for My kingdom. Do not fret or worry, for your loved ones are in My hands. They are gently being guided in the way they should go. Continue to pray for them."

April 21

Thus saith the Lord;

"You are the light of the world. You are My eyes, ears, mouth, and hands. I will use you in many ways. You are My precious child, in whom I rejoice. You bring Me much pleasure. *Rejoice!* My hand is upon you. Everything you put your hands to do will be blessed."

April 22

Thus saith the Lord;

"Follow your heart, for where your heart is, your treasure will be also. Continue to love those that I send across your path. You will see changes and answers to prayers—you will rejoice."

April 23

Thus saith the Lord;

"Love Me with your whole heart, mind, and soul. Your reward shall be great. You shall see My glory come. You will rejoice and be exceedingly glad. Your willingness to help and give to others has not gone unnoticed. You will be blessed. You will be like me—a strong tower and many will run to you. I love you and you are mine."

April 24

Thus saith the Lord;

"To know that you are blessed is one thing; to feel that you are blessed is another thing; and to see that you are blessed is still another thing. You must first know that you are blessed. When you know this, you will then feel that you are blessed. When you know and feel that you are blessed, you will then see how blessed you are. It is a spiritual walk of faith. I work from the inside out: first with the heart, then the mind, then the eyes. My child you surely will be blessed."

April 25

Thus saith the Lord;

"How anointed are your prayers. They smell as sweet incense to My nose. You shall receive all that you ask for. Be careful what you ask for. You are My blessed child in whom I am well-pleased. Your journey has been continually upward. The climb is not always easy. Remember, one step at a time—resting along the way. Progress is the key and I see much progress. Your faith shall be rewarded. Do not lose hope, do not grow weary, for I shall be your strength and I will be everything that you need."

April 26

Thus saith the Lord;

"Look to Me for your every need. I am the Almighty Guide, Help, and Supplier. I give all good gifts. I give wealth, health, and life. I am all you need. You must believe that all things are possible with Me, for he that believes shall receive. Continue to seek Me for all things. I am a rewarder of those who diligently seek Me."

April 27

Thus saith the Lord;

"Give this day unto Me. Let Me help you along your way. Think of Me and talk to Me often. Take time in your busy life to commune with Me. I will help you with all you need to do. Offer Me your troubles, cares, and concerns, and I will offer you solutions to help you through. You will feel My peace. You will feel My love. You will feel My guidance. I am always here. I am always near. I love you."

April 28

Thus saith the Lord;

"I am the way, the life and the truth. No one comes to the Father except through Me. I will bless those who diligently seek Me and their reward will be great. In due time, you shall reap. Now is the time to sow."

April 29

Thus saith the Lord;

"Above all things, My child, learn patience. Do not be anxious for anything, but by prayer and supplication, let your requests be made known to Me. Then you must trust and know that I will answer you in the best possible way and at the appropriate time. It will be My way and in My time. The results will benefit you greatly because My interests are for you—only the best gifts for My children. Knowing this, can you wait patiently for my perfect gifts? Be patient and wait, be peaceful and joyful—knowing that I care for you and that I am in control. The best is yet to come."

April 30

Thus saith the Lord;

"I love you and I am all you need. I need you. Do not worry, My child, I will guide you by My eye. I shall provide all your needs. I will be your friend and commune with you."

MAY

Let your light so shine before men, that they may see
your good works and glorify your Father in heaven.

Matthew 5:16

May 1

Thus saith the Lord;

"How your light does shine. Many will be drawn to Me by your light. So let your light shine more. Your joy will be full."

May 2

Thus saith the Lord;

"Be at peace with the world and all people, especially in situations that you have no control over. Lift others up to Me in prayer and let My work be accomplished. All power has been given to Me. I can change the hearts of men; I can change the course of the world. Do this and you can have My peace. My peace is like none the world can give. You can have this peace by entrusting to Me what you love, care for, and are concerned about. I will take good care of what you give Me as long as you don't take it back. I will not lose it or break it, and I will give it back to you in better condition than when I got it. Trust Me and My peace will be yours."

May 3

Thus saith the Lord;

"Let your heart not be troubled or afraid. Let My peace rule and reign in your heart. Do you still not know that I am in control? You are not your own. You have been bought with a price. Let Me fight your battles. For the battles belong to Me. I shall conquer. I shall win. Victory belongs to Me. You must let Me accomplish My work. Trust Me."

May 4

Thus saith the Lord;

"I will tell you the things that you need to know. I will show you the things that you need to see. I will take you where you need to be. No man is perfect. Do not be harsh on another's faults and imperfections, unless the same judgment is granted to you. Let Me be the judge. Let Me deal with the sins of another man. Your only responsibility is to pray and keep My commandments. Let him without sin cast the first stone."

May 5

Thus saith the Lord;

"My child, My work is a life-long process. My work never ceases. My work is never done. There is so much work to be done. Laborers are few, but the work is plenty. Do not expect changes overnight. Certainly it is possible, for I can accomplish anything. I created the whole earth in six days. You will see changes—most of which will be gradual—but everlasting. You have much to be thankful for. Happiness is a choice. Choose to be happy."

May 6

Thus saith the Lord;

"You are very special to Me. I know your heart and mind. I cherish the times we have together just as you cherish the times together with the ones you love. Insecurity is a fear. I have not given you the spirit of fear, but of power and love and a sound mind. Repeat this whenever you feel insecure. Continue to pray for your needs, wants, and desires. Continue to pray for those you love. Remember you cannot alter the plans I have for you, as long as you are with Me. Do not fear, but rejoice, for I am doing a glorious work and you will be blessed."

May 7

Thus saith the Lord;

"You are My beloved child, in whom I am well-pleased. You bring Me much joy. Your prayers are as sweet incense to My throne and there is much more that I will show to you and give to you. It is My great pleasure to give you great gifts. Look up to heaven and rejoice, for I am your Lord God and you are My child. I hear your prayers and I am at work. My work never ceases. I never grow weary and I do not sleep. It is almost the season for you to reap. Your blessings shall be like the stars in the sky. You are precious in My eyes. Do not fret or worry, for I am in control and I have great and mighty plans for your life."

May 8

Thus saith the Lord;

"Have no fear, for nothing comes your way that I do not allow. See the good in all things. Try to find good in all things, in every person and every situation."

May 9

Thus saith the Lord;

"Watch—watch and pray. Be alert concerning what is going on around you. Be spiritually minded. Distinguish whether it is Me or the enemy. Then act accordingly. If it is I, you will feel peace, love, and joy. If it is the enemy you need to pray for peace, love, and joy. I will be there for you. I will fight your battles. Your battles belong to Me and you will have the victory, saith the Lord. By doing this you will maintain your peace, love, and joy."

May 10

Thus saith the Lord;

"Your sadness will be turned into joy—your sorrow to gladness. Do not fret over the little things. Remember this life is just temporal and life in the eternal will be spent with Me. I am always with you. Say My name often and you will feel Me. I will be near you. I can fulfill your every need. I will be closer to you than a brother, mother, or a friend. I will never let you down, but I will lift you up with My two hands. Do not fret or worry, for they accomplish nothing. They only steal and rob your joy. I hear your prayers and I will answer them in the best and quickest way possible. Your prayers to Me are of greater value than money. I delight in you, My child, and your faith will be rewarded. I love you more than you love your own children."

May 11

Thus saith the Lord;

"Hearts can be softened by My touch. Hearts can be repaired by My healing touch. Eyes can be opened by My hands. Thinking can be changed by My Spirit. Thoughts can be transformed by My thoughts. Minds can be renewed by My Spirit. Spirits can be re-birthed by My Spirit."

May 12

Thus saith the Lord;

"Be ready for what is about to happen. You have been patient and have endured much. Miracles are being released. You shall have those things that you have asked for. My blessings shall overcome you. Your desires shall manifest. Your needs shall perish. Your sadness will turn to joy. You have been faithful in little; continue to be faithful in a lot. I am your Lord, your God, and you are My beloved child in whom I am well-pleased."

May 13

Thus saith the Lord;

"My precious child, life is like a school. It is a learning classroom. Each day I teach you a new thing. Take hold of these things and use them and I will teach you many, many more things. Many mighty things are about to come. You will abound in spiritual blessings and material blessings. These blessings have begun."

May 14

Thus saith the Lord;

"I am teaching you many spiritual truths. Mighty powers are unfolding before your eyes. You have the power to conquer and the power to overcome. You have won many spiritual battles. I am very pleased with your progress. Wonders are unfolding. You shall be a blessing to many. My blessings shall pour out to you and yours."

May 15

Thus saith the Lord;

"I am so glad when you come to Me and commune with Me. Come to Me often. For it is My great pleasure to spend time with you and talk with you. It makes Me smile to see you smile. I feel what you feel. Do not worry about your future. Your future is in My hands. I am in control. I am your God. You are My child. I love you and you bring Me much joy. I am making My desires your desires. I am doing many mighty things in your life. You have already begun to see these things. It is just the beginning. For you will see many, many, mighty works throughout your life. Your prayers are being answered. Your prayers are mighty and powerful. Continue to pray. Continue to learn. I will teach you many things—and all things will continue to grow: your faith, My power in your life, your knowledge, wisdom, and your spirit."

May 16

Thus saith the Lord;

"If you have faith of a mustard seed you can move a mountain. All have been given a measure of faith. Then faith increases: faith comes by hearing and hearing by the Word of God. Do not doubt, for all is possible to him who believes. You must first believe in your heart to see with your eyes. This is contrary to the world's view, that seeing is believing. I say believe and then you will see it."

May 17

Thus saith the Lord;

"My precious child, you desire joy, unspeakable joy. Seek and you shall find. Joy is one of My greater gifts. It is a gift and is freely given by Me. This gift has to be used and maintained by you and that is where the problem lies. I will teach you how to maintain your joy. Begin to study joy. Learn what My Word says about joy. Know that when this joy is obtained and maintained, that mighty things will happen in My kingdom. Joy will spread to others. Joy is the devil's worst enemy. Joy produces singing. Joy produces worship. Joy produces dancing. Just think what an outbreak of joy will produce in your church! This is good, My child, and I am very glad that you asked and are seeking. You shall be blessed. A ripple effect is produced from joy."

Joy—Isaiah 12:3
"Therefore with joy you will draw water from the wells of salvation."

May 18

Thus saith the Lord;

"Continue in My Words, for they are life to your flesh and health to your bones. I came that you might have life more abundantly. Continue in Me and you shall have this abundant life. You are on the brink of a miracle. I love you, My precious child. You bring Me much joy. I love these times together. Do not fear, for I am always with you. I see your heart."

May 19

Thus saith the Lord;

"Be assured that I am at work, that I am in control, and that I love you very much."

May 20

Thus saith the Lord;

"I would have you know that mighty things are being accomplished through you for My kingdom. Many people see your shining light. People whom you do not even know are watching you: in the market places, in public places, at your work, in your church. They see a special glow about you. You are My child and you are special to Me."

May 21

Thus saith the Lord;

"Do not feel like you have to do a lot for Me to make Me happy. Some people are too busy. Even *Jesus* took time to be alone with Me. I have said there is a lot of work to be done, but I did not mean that only a few would do all of the work. Pray for more laborers. When help is needed, let others know. You must have rest time in Me and spend time with Me. You need times of refreshing, alone time, and you-and-Me time. You need growing time in My Word and faith building time in prayer with Me. I do not give you more than you can handle, and if you are too busy to spend time with Me, then adjustments should be made. Give Me the first part of your day, and then I will leave plenty of time left for you and your responsibilities. I will even help you accomplish them."

May 22

Thus saith the Lord;

"I am the way, the life, and the truth. No man comes to the Father, but through Me. No works originating from self-count for My kingdom. Many do good things, but do not know Me. They seek to impress others; their motive is people-pleasing. They will come to Me in the end and say 'Lord, Lord, I have done this or that,' and I will say to them—*GO, for I do not even know you*. Do not keep them in your company, lest they bring you down with them."

May 23

Thus saith the Lord;

"My hand is mighty to save. Do not give up praying for the lost. Pray that ministering angels would be sent to them, that they might see the light and go toward the light. I am the light of the world. Be their friend and help point the way. Ask Me to lead you. I will show you what to do, for you will be My tool to lead the way for many. I desire to see all men and women saved. I want to see families saved. I want to see cities saved. I want to see nations saved. My heart cries out for the whole world that My Father has given to Me. Thank you for your faithfulness to Me. I love you."

May 24

Thus saith the Lord;

"My hand is not too short to save. I desire that all come to salvation. That is why I sent My beloved Son: that whosoever would believe in Him would be saved. Repent and be baptized every one of you. You must die to your old life and be raised anew. Now, rejoice in your salvation. It is free to anyone who asks, for by grace you were saved."

May 25

Thus saith the Lord;

"When life's storms are raging all around you, remember that you can take shelter with your Lord, your God, and your Redeemer. I will hide you under My wing. I will guide and protect you. Stay calm and know that I am in control. I will walk through the storm with you. Sometimes the storm will cease and other times it will continue to rage. *Have faith!* Just as each day comes to an end, the trials that you are going through will also come to an end. Try to learn from these trying times. Stay close to Me and I will comfort you. Pray that My will is done and then let Me do My work. Put all in My hands and trust Me."

May 26

Thus saith the Lord;

"My will and My plan for your life will not always work out in the way that you think that it should. You pray for My will to be done. Is that what you want: My will or your will to be done in your life? Which one do you want? If you want My will to be done then you will have to step aside and let Me accomplish those things that I need to do to get you there. Sometimes it is painful. You will not always like it, but the end result will be more glorious than you could ever imagine. Let's do it My way."

May 27

Thus saith the Lord;

"The spiritual walk is like the four seasons. There are dry seasons when really not much is accomplished because you are rather distant from Me. There are hot seasons where you are on fire for Me, and there is much growth. There are cold seasons where growth has slowed and practically stopped. There are rainy seasons when much of My Spirit is poured out on you. I desire that you stay hot and that the rain pours down on you. Where are you today?"

May 28

Thus saith the Lord;

"No matter how bad you think that your problem is, you can always find someone who has a problem much worse. Do not dwell on your own problems, but rather try to help someone get a victory over their problems; by doing this, you will also begin to get a victory over your problems—you both will be blessed! Find something to be thankful for every day. Before you know it, it will become a habit. A thankful heart is a happy heart."

May 29

Thus saith the Lord;

"I am doing a new thing in your heart and mind today. You are becoming more like Me every day. The things that I love, you will love. Those I care about, you will care about. The things that break My heart, will break your heart. The things that I hate, you will hate. I am renewing you and transforming your heart and mind to be more like Me. My will is being accomplished in your life. You cannot see all the changes that are being made, but rest assured I am doing a mighty work. My work does not cease. I never grow weary. I do not sleep. Be patient My child, soon you will even see as I see. I love you—now be blessed."

May 30

Thus saith the Lord;

"Fear is not from Me, for I have not given you the spirit of fear, but of power and of love and a sound mind. Cast out fear, rebuke it and it will flee from you. Fear keeps you from doing My work: it is crippling and paralyzing. Do not be afraid, for I am with you. Instead, dwell in My love, by My side, and let My love pour through you. My love will cover a multitude of sins. By My stripes you were healed, by My stripes you were forgiven, and by My blood you have been washed as white as snow. You have nothing to be afraid of; if I am for you, who can be against you?"

May 31

Thus saith the Lord;

"Live each day like there is no tomorrow, for you do not know what tomorrow may bring. Greet one another with a holy kiss. Be kind and loving toward others. Do unto others as you would have them do unto you, for this is My commandment. Seek not your own pleasure, but try to bring pleasure to others. Try to make someone else's day brighter, more joyful, and their load lighter. You must become as a servant, without complaining. Just as I came to serve, you must also learn to serve. Your reward will be great in heaven."

JUNE

These things I command you, that you love one another.

John 15:17

June 1

Thus saith the Lord;

"Even when you do not feel like loving, I command you to love. When you do not feel like giving, I command you to give. When you do not feel like you can forgive, I say forgive. Do not trust your feelings, for they cannot be trusted. Trust only in Me. Live only for Me. My ways are higher than your ways. My thoughts are higher than your thoughts. Once you have given your problems to Me, do not take them back because your feelings will cause you to stumble. Entrust them with Me and I will bring a most satisfying solution to your problem. I have said so—so let it be. Will you trust Me?"

June 2

Thus saith the Lord;

"You must be careful that when My blessings come, and all is well, that you do not try to leave the Promised Land. Blessings are coming and your storehouse will be full, but you must not leave My side or all could perish and be taken away. Many have the tendency to forget about Me when everything seems to be going well. Instead, use this time to help others and be thankful. The more you give, the more you shall receive. This is My spiritual law. I will send those to you who are in need and those who need your prayers. I am making you as a strong tower. Be blessed so that those around you shall also be blessed."

June 3

Thus saith the Lord;

"I am leading you to fast and pray. Sometimes when you pray and pray and seem to not obtain that which you are seeking, you must put on the armor that I have given you. These are: the breast plate of righteousness; the shield of faith; and the helmet of salvation. You have to pound the gates of hell in My name: use My name

(*Jesus*). Come against that which torments you or your loved ones. Pray and fast. Seek Me! Praise and worship Me! I will send an army with you and together the enemy shall be conquered—he must flee. Strongholds will be broken. Stand on My Word. Stand in awe. I have defeated the enemy and the gates of hell shall not prevail against you!"

June 4

Thus saith the Lord;

"Let us enter His gates with thanksgiving and praise. Let us worship our King, for He is worthy of our praise; He reigns in power and glory. Find something to be happy about today and every day. Before you know it, a fountain shall spring up through your being; and I say such a joy will arise that nothing, and I mean nothing, can take that joy from you. You have much to be thankful for, regardless of what you think. *Search for it!* Soon searching will not be needed; it will be natural to give thanks. I reign on high and someday you will reign with Me—until then, live. Live in peace and live in joy. I am coming again. Where I go, you will go with Me."

June 5

Thus saith the Lord;

"Train children in the ways of the Lord and when they are old, they will not depart from them. They may stumble and fall, but their ways are ordered by Me. If they have departed from Me, pray for their safe and fast return. Pray that no harm would come to them, because while they are wandering from Me, they are not under My net of protection, unless you cover them in prayer. They are as one of My lost sheep that I will seek and return to My fold. They will eventually return to Me."

June 6

Thus saith the Lord;

"Many will be sent across your path that I desire to touch. You will be My instrument. Do whatsoever I tell you to do. It may be a kind word, a smile, a hug, money and, of course, prayer. They need to see Me in you. I will not ask anything of you that I have not already equipped you to do. You are going to see lives transformed, souls saved, many healed, and mighty works done by Me for My kingdom's sake. Not by power, not by might, but by My Spirit. Be not afraid concerning what you will speak because I will give you the words to speak. I have already established the outcome because I go before you and prepare the way. You are to set My plan into motion."

June 7

Thus saith the Lord;

"Fight the good fight of faith, for faith comes by hearing and hearing by the Word of God. Pray that your faith would increase. It is impossible to please God without faith. With faith you can move mountains; faith believes that you have received what you have asked for before you actually receive it. Great faith is hard to acquire. Strive for it. I need faith-filled believers to do the work that I did, and greater works than these can they do because I have gone to My Father who is in heaven. Do you not know that unbelief is sin? So pray for more faith and be in My Word."

June 8

Thus saith the Lord;

"As far as the east is from the west is how great My love is for you. Great is the love of the Father. There are no words to describe My love for you. I will pour out My love to you in great measure. My compassion is on you and those you love. Love is more than a feeling. It is a commandment: that you love one another, even as I have loved you, and love your neighbor as yourself. If you love, therefore, forgive also. You must forgive others in order to be forgiven by Me. Try to love all that I bring across your path. Do not judge, for by what measure you judge others, you also will be judged by Me. Let love rule your heart."

June 9

Thus saith the Lord;

"Store up your treasure in heaven and not on this earth. Where I am you will be there with Me, and your rewards will be in heaven and not on earth. Do not have more than what you need, and if you do have more than what you need, give some away. Verily I say to you, it is easier for a camel to go through the eye of a needle than for a rich man to enter into heaven. Be wise and diligent over your money and possessions. Do not let the lusts of worldly possessions be your focus, for it is in Me that you move and have your being. All good and perfect gifts come down from the Father who is in heaven. Be content with what you have. Love Me more than life itself and all will be well between you and My Father."

June 10

Thus saith the Lord;

"Just as each day is a new day, so is the work for My kingdom. Spring forth with a new joy in the morning, because I will have a new thing for you; something new to teach you; something new to reveal to you; something new for you to do for Me. Seek Me and My ways, and I will reveal many mighty things to you. Sing a new song. Hum a new tune. Meet someone new today. My work will not be hard. I just need willing hearts and obedient servants to do all that I ask. You reward will be great. You will develop a deeper relationship with Me. It will be a trusting relationship unlike that found with any human being. Come to Me all you that are heavily burdened, and I will give you rest."

June 11

Thus saith the Lord;

"My hand is upon you and all that you do. Whatsoever you do, do it in love and do it in My name. I go before you and prepare your way. Your footsteps are ordered by Me. I open doors where you should go, and I close doors where you should not go. Do not get disappointed when your plans do not happen the way that you think they should. I am gently directing you another way. I know the plans that I have for you. They are good and you will be happy. *Cheer up! Have faith and trust Me!* After all, you are a child of a KING."

June 12

Thus saith the Lord;

Do not be afraid to do for others and to buy gifts for others. Gifts are all part of giving, and I love a cheerful giver. When you give to others you also give to Me. Do not worry for I know your heart and your motives. Give and it shall be given to you. Also, it is better to give than to receive. If I motivate you to buy and to give, than rest assured I will provide for you. Just be obedient. So give—give and be blessed."

June 13

Thus saith the Lord;

"There will be times of refreshing. There will be growing times, alone times, sad times and joyful times. They all must come. There are cleansing times and intimate times. Your walk will be ever changing, going anywhere you allow it. I do My part but you must do your part. I will never leave you nor forsake you. I will be here every time you call. Just call and I will be there. My thoughts are continually with you, for I love you. I stand in the gap and am always before My Father on your behalf. Draw close to Me, and I will draw close to you. I desire to be everything to you. I am everything that you need. I bless you."

June 14

Thus saith the Lord;

"My work is ongoing. Let Me do My work and I will show you what you are to do. My work is not always visible; I begin on the inside with the heart and the mind. You cannot see this work until the outward transformation begins. Though you do not see My inner workings, this does not mean that I am not working. Have faith, believe, and remember all of the things that I have told you. Cease not to pray for the things that you desire. Do not give up hope or grow weary. You will see answers to your prayers. In due time, you shall reap."

June 15

Thus saith the Lord;

"I shall perfect that which I have made. I am molding and fashioning you into My image. Growing pains are uncomfortable and often come in spurts. Continue to pray. You cannot change the plans that I have for you. You can only delay them."

June 16

Thus saith the Lord;

"Come, all of you that are burdened and I will give you rest. Commune with Me! Tell Me your problems and I will help you. I will give you solutions to your problems. I can help. I will make your load lighter so you won't have to carry so much. I will lead the way and all you have to do is follow. I will uphold you with My mighty hand. You are not alone. I can turn a terrible situation around to something good and wonderful. Come unto Me. Give Me your all and I will give you rest. You must trust Me, My child. Be as trusting as a small child and take that leap of faith."

June 17

Thus saith the Lord;

"I am the way, the truth, and the life. No one comes to the Father except through Me. He that believes in Me shall have life, abundant life. He that believes in Me and the works that I do shall he do also, and greater works than these because I go to My Father. There is power in My name. There is healing in My name. Miracles will come in My name. Use My name often, *Jesus*. There is no greater name under heaven or on the earth than the name of *Jesus*. Demons will flee when they hear My name. Curses will be broken by My name. **Speak My name! Say My name!** Power will come when the name of *Jesus* is spoken. Learn to speak positively because there is power in all your words. You have the power to bless or to curse. Read the Word; speak the Word; live the Word; for I AM the Living Word."

June 18

Thus saith the Lord;

"Do not judge others. How can you say a person is doing something wrong when you do things that are wrong? Try to improve yourself and lift your concerns for others to Me. I will be the judge. Let not your heart be troubled. Believe in Me and the things that I have said. Soon, the clouds will disappear, and the sun will come out and shine. Soon all will be well. Can you say all is well? Tomorrow will be a new day. It will be like a new beginning. Start each day fresh and try to make each day better. You are growing stronger and wiser. **Rejoice!** Again, I say **rejoice!**"

June 19

Thus saith the Lord;

"My Spirit is moving, not only in your life, but in the lives of all believers that are seeking Me and My will. I am moving across the nations—across the world. I am doing a new thing like never before. I am preparing My army. I am strengthening My people. They shall stand victorious. They shall stand before Me in awe. Every knee shall bow and every tongue shall confess that *Jesus* is Lord. You shall be with Me forevermore."

June 20

Thus saith the Lord;

"Although you may have dark times and it may seem as though I have left you, rest assured that I have not. I will never leave you nor forsake you. It is not I, but rather you, who are slipping away. Spend time with Me; read My Word; commune with Me; and spend alone time with Me. You must separate yourself from the world and find a quiet place each and every day or else the busy world will consume you. Slow down, spend time with Me, and everything else will fall into place. I love you and I need you too."

June 21

Thus saith the Lord;

"Do not be angry. Do not be jealous. Do not lie. Do not fear. All of these will steal your joy and My love cannot flow through you. These are all fiery darts from the enemy. They are sent to kill, steal and destroy. When one of these feelings arises in your spirit, you must rebuke it and send it right back from where it came from. I am training you. You must learn these lessons. Soon there will be nothing; I mean nothing that the devil can throw at you to cause you to stumble. He is a defeated foe."

June 22

Thus saith the Lord;

"Someone needs you today. Be a friend to someone today. Try to cheer someone up and make their day a little brighter. Be kind and say something nice. Give a hug. Touch someone's hand or arm today. Be attentive. Listen to or encourage someone today. They have come to you this day because they see Me in you and they desire what you have. Be that bridge. Stand in the gap for them. You never know, they might not be here tomorrow. Do not put off until tomorrow what you can do today."

June 23

Thus saith the Lord;

"This is the day that I have made. Rejoice and be glad in it. Each day that comes to you is a gift from Me. I created all things for you to enjoy. See My beauty all around you. Salvation has come to your house this day. Your faithful prayers have been answered. It has been written that you and your household shall be saved. They shall all abide satisfied and will lack nothing. The two shall become one flesh and will rule and reign with Me. Do not let the sun go down on your wrath. Always kiss before bed. Love him more than yourself and love her more than yourself. Be each other's helper. Do not esteem yourself more than the other, but be equal. May your love grow stronger as you grow in Me! For two are better than one, and where two are gathered in My name, there I am in the midst of them. *Rejoice, My children! Rejoice!*"

June 24

Thus saith the Lord;

"I never said this would be easy. The concept is simple because even children have the faith to believe, for everyone that believes in Me shall be saved. The walk can be difficult at times. That is why I tell you that I am with you, will guide you, and help you along the way. Everyone who hates Me will hate you because I live in you. Do not despair. The enemy will come against you, but stand strong in your faith. The devil is a defeated foe and no harm shall come to you. Rejoice in your salvation because the day draws near when I will return and take you with Me to spend eternity together."

June 25

Thus saith the Lord;

"There are many things that you need to learn. It is like starting school all over again. Do not expect to skip from kindergarten to twelfth grade in a few months. It is a growing process, like a baby who first desires only milk. As the baby grows and gets older; then the child can eat meat. Your walk with Me is the same. First, you are carried, then you crawl, then you can walk and finally you can run. There is much to learn. Continue daily with Me, and I will teach you all things. I do not expect you to pass every test the first time. I am patient and desire to teach you. You will accomplish much for My kingdom. My protection I give to you—so live. *Live and Learn!*"

June 26

Thus saith the Lord;

"Everything that you do, do it joyfully and for Me. A merry heart makes Me glad. I desire that your joy should be full. Do not let the enemy steal your joy. He is a liar and a thief. He will try everything to steal your joy. Protect your joy like you would protect your earthly belongings. Keep it under lock and key. The lock is your heart and the key is My name, *Jesus*. No man can steal this joy from you, but only you can let it go. Remember the things I have told you. Put your trust in Me. Keep the strong faith and believe. Do not doubt, stand strong, pursue Me and My ways and all things will be added to you."

June 27

Thus saith the Lord;

"Delight yourself in Me and I will give you the desires of your heart. It is My great privilege and deep desire to give you good gifts. I am a giver and that is what I came for: to give you forgiveness, to give you love, to give you a purpose, and to give you a better life. I came to give you an abundant life. I desire that you prosper in everything you do. When you are happy, I am happy also. Desire to do good things for others, just as you would have Me do good things for you. If each person did one kind act for another, the whole world would feel the ripple effect of kindness."

June 28

Thus saith the Lord;

"You are My beloved child, in whom I am well-pleased. Your praise and worship is as sweet incense to Me. Your beautiful spirit is pleasing to My eye. My delight is in you. I am grateful for all of your prayers—prayers for yourself and others. I am excited to answer them all. I love the time that you spend with Me. You are a friend indeed. Expect a miracle. Look for Me everywhere today. Feel My presence throughout the day because I am with you."

June 29

Thus saith the Lord;

"I want to encourage you to continue in My Word and in prayer even though you do not feel like progress is being made. Not only am I doing mighty works in the lives of your loved ones, I am also doing a mighty work in your life. You pray for them to be changed, but it is you also whom I am changing. Be patient. First, seek the change in your own life."

June 30

Thus saith the Lord;

"When I give you a thought or put a desire in your heart to do something, be confident and do that thing, for I go before you and prepare your way. I give you the strength and the will to accomplish the thing that I have asked of you. Do not fear, do not think, do not question, just be obedient and do that which I have asked you to do. You will not always understand, but it is important that you obey, for there is a reason—by obeying, something miraculous will happen. It may not be visible or even comprehendible. There is a spiritual realm all around you and if it were visible, you would understand more. I need willing hearts and obedient minds, here on earth, to help accomplish My will. Thank you for being an important part of My ministry. I love you and nothing can separate My love from you."

JULY

So then faith comes by hearing, and hearing by
the Word of God.

Romans 10:17

July 1

Thus saith the Lord;

"When you pray and ask for something—anything—especially healing in My name (*Jesus*), believe that you receive it. Even if you do not see it or feel it, you must still believe. That is what faith is. Faith believes that you receive it before you actually receive it. To receive My greatest gifts you will have to receive them by faith. They will come! Believe it and then you will receive it. Faith comes by hearing and hearing by the Word of God. Learn it, love it, and live it. Pray that your faith would increase. Yes, pray for more faith. Indeed you will have those things that you ask for."

July 2

Thus saith the Lord;

"Children are one of our greatest blessings. You are My child and I am greatly blessed when you desire to spend time with Me. You need not always come asking or wanting. I desire a closer relationship—a relationship where you tell Me everything. Yes, I am your God, your Father, your Maker, your Creator, and I also want to be your friend. I want to be a friend that you can trust and rely on. Open up your heart and mind to Me today and let Me be that friend to you."

July 3

Thus saith the Lord;

"My peace I give to you—a peace in your inner man—a calmness knowing that I am with you and taking care of you—a peace knowing that you can trust Me and know that I am in control. This is a peace where you will know that I love you and have all power; this peace passes all understanding. With this peace you will know you are forgiven and will spend eternity with Me. Breathe this peace, live this peace, rest in this peace. I am your God and you are My child."

July 4

Thus saith the Lord;

"Delight yourself in Me and I will give you the desires of your heart. Every good and perfect gift comes from the Father above. Whatsoever things you ask for in My name (*Jesus*), believe that you receive them and you shall have them. I reward those who diligently seek Me. I desire that you may prosper in all things and be in health, just as your soul prospers. Do good and be a cheerful giver, for when you give to someone in need you also give to Me. Give and it will be given to you in greater measure."

July 5

Thus saith the Lord;

"Miracles are coming! Healings are coming! Restorations are coming! I am pouring out My Spirit on all flesh and blood. For everyone who asks, they shall receive. I have come that you might have life, yes, and a more abundant life. Do not turn back. No, you cannot go back. I will give you a new life. I will give you a new identity. The old will be gone and all things will be new. Continue in Me and I will continue to do the good work that I have begun in you. Rejoice and be exceedingly glad, for you have heard the good news."

July 6

Thus saith the Lord;

"Hide My Word in your heart so that you may not sin against Me. Put a song in your mind, that your joy may be full. Lift up the problems of others and your load will be lighter as well. Give money to the poor so your needs will be met. Be a friend to someone so that you will have a friend. There is a required action to be taken for every blessing that you are seeking. If you want a friend, you must be a friend. If you need money, you must be a giver. If you want to be loved, you must be able to love. The spiritual law is not at all like the worldly law. Whatever it is that you pray for and seek; ask Me to reveal what you must do to receive this. Often times you will only have to believe. What is it that you are seeking today?"

July 7

Thus saith the Lord;

"My never ending supply of love is available to you at all times. It should flow like a river through you to others. Many are thirsty but will not drink. You must be the bridge between them and Me. Lead them to the river for a sip. They will see Me in you and desire what you have. Do as I say, follow as I lead, and allow Me to do the rest."

July 8

Thus saith the Lord;

"My people are to be a praising people, a worshipping people. My children are to be thankful and welcoming. They shall be an expectant and a giving people. That is right; you are to expect to receive, for what you give away you shall receive back multiplied. Expect to receive from Me. I am your Lord and your God. I am merciful and am a rewarder of those who diligently seek Me. Expect great things for there is nothing too hard for Me to accomplish. Nothing is impossible for Me. Enlarge you vision. You must first be able to see it to receive it."

July 9

Thus saith the Lord;

"My army is growing bigger. My army is growing stronger. The enemy will come, but the enemy cannot stand against you, for if I am for you who can be against you? No weapon formed against you shall prosper. Do not fear! He who is in you is greater than he who is in the world. *Rejoice! Praise!* Praise can make the walls fall down. Praise will open the windows from heaven to flood the believer with

His divine Spirit. Do not grow weary. Do not faint—in due time you shall reap."

July 10

Thus saith the Lord;

"I am your God Almighty, the Everlasting, the Faithful and Just, the Alpha and Omega, Creator of the universe and the One whom you seek. I am a very present help in your time of trouble. I am very near and I do hear every prayer. I hear your cries and I give you new mercies every day. I am working out perfect solutions to all of your problems and concerns. Allow My will to be done. Be patient. Answers are coming. You shall see a breakthrough because you have been diligently praying for an answer. Continue to do the things that I have told you to do and you will be in My will. I will lead you and guide you. Stay close to Me so that your joy may be full. I am all that you need. I will see you through and be with you until the end. *Rejoice!*"

July 11

Thus saith the Lord;

"The moment that you ask Me to forgive you—that very moment—it is done and I remember it no more. Do not dwell on the thing that you did. You must also forget it. This faith principal is one of the easier ones to believe. The truth is that each and every request that you ask of Me should be as easy to believe. Let that sink into your spirit because you only need faith the size of a mustard seed to move a mountain. Do you have any mountains in your life today? Ask of Me, believe that it is done and then forget it. Believe that the very moment you asked—it was accomplished by Me. You know and believe that when you ask Me to forgive you, I do. Have that same faith for *everything* that you ask for."

July 12

Thus saith the Lord;

"Do not attempt to save the world on your own. Wait upon the Lord. I will lead you. I will open the doors where you should go and close the doors where you should not go. When a door closes, it does not always mean 'no'. It may be that the time is 'not now'. There is a time and a season for everything: a time to prepare the ground, a time to sow the seed, a time to water, and a time of harvest. Pray for more laborers. Pray for an abundant harvest."

July 13

Thus saith the Lord;

"I will take care of you. I will provide your every need. Do not worry about your future because I am in control. Do not be anxious because I will reveal each step to you at the precise moment. You will not be led astray. You know My voice and you will follow Me all the days of your life. So be content: full of hope and joyful, knowing that the One who knows all cares for you. Give Me all of your stress from trying to figure everything out on your own, because we are going to do it My way. I have a plan. Wait on Me and I will show you My perfect plan."

July 14

Thus saith the Lord;

"Try one day without worrying about anything. When a worry creeps in, hand it to Me and leave it at My altar. I will gladly take care of whatever it may be. Then you will have more time to focus on Me and My work. Whatever it is that distracts you from My work is My problem also. Surrender it to Me so I can work out a solution. I promise to give you an answer and a solution to whatever hinders you. Your answer may or may not come quickly, but you must trust that I am working out the best possible way to handle it. I love you and I need you more than you need Me. I created you because I need your love, companionship, and worship. In return, I will give you My kingdom."

July 15

Thus saith the Lord;

"You are not here by luck or chance. You were planned by Me. You were created to serve a specific purpose as My child. I formed you in your mother's womb and I know the beginning until the end. Everything that you have done or will do, I knew about before it happened. I have a plan for your life. Choose My plan and My way and I promise you that your life will be full. Reflect on those things that have already happened. Can you see My hand on them? No matter what you are going through today, know that I am there with you and My hand is upon it. No, you probably can't see it now, but you will later. *Trust Me! Trust Me!*"

July 16

Thus saith the Lord;

"I desire to have an intimate relationship with you—the kind of relationship where you are totally in love with Me—one that I am all that you think of all day long. Be devoted and entrusted to Me. I want you to commune with Me and share everything with Me. I want to spend every moment of the day and night with you. I will love you unconditionally. I will comfort you. I will help you. I will provide for your every need. I will never leave you. I will lift you up. I will bring you joy. I will lead you. I will commune with you. I will help make your load lighter. I will protect you. You love Me because I have first loved you. Your love for Me is growing and I love that."

July 17

Thus saith the Lord;

"I hear your prayers and supplications. They are as a sweet offering to Me. The moment that you pray, the spiritual realm springs forth into action. Your prayers are as spoken permission to set My plans into action. Remember, unless I am asked and given permission, I can do nothing. Anything that you ask, according to My will, I will do for you. My Spirit lives in you and will bring things to your mind. Lift these in prayer. I will make your heart break with the things that make My heart break. Lift these in prayer. I will bring people across your path. Lift these people in prayer. The things that you hear—lift in prayer. The things that you see—lift in prayer. My people are to be a praying people. The world can be changed through prayer, so pray without ceasing."

July 18

Thus saith the Lord;

"You must look for the good in everyone, for you cannot judge a book by its cover. Beauty is only skin deep and the real beauty is what is inside. The eyes are the windows to the soul. The heart houses the Spirit. The mind thinks and speaks from the Spirit. You will know Me by My Spirit. Release My Spirit through prayer to those without My Spirit so that I may minister to them. I am bringing those across your path that do not have My Spirit. Release My love to them."

July 19

Thus saith the Lord;

"When your focus and attention are on Me then nothing else should matter. Turn all of your priorities to heavenly priorities, kingly priorities, spiritual priorities, and all of your earthly priorities will fall into place and will also be provided for. Seek first My kingdom and righteousness and all things will be added to you. We are in a battle and we are running a race. Think of it this way: when you are in a battle you do not stop fighting. You do not put your guard down. You must continue to take ground. Do not rest comfortably for long. Instead, put on the full armor and stand ready, willing and able. The Lord is coming soon."

July 20

Thus saith the Lord;

"You will be amazed to know what a difference you are making for My kingdom. Do not believe the lies of the enemy. The day will come when you stand before Me at My judgment seat and you will hear Me say, 'well done My faithful servant' and I will flash before your eyes what your faithfulness and prayers have done to advance My kingdom—you will be amazed. Do not think that you are not valuable to Me. I have called you as a son or a daughter and I have an inheritance for you. You are an heir and you shall receive your inheritance."

July 21

Thus saith the Lord;

"You are not here by chance! It was pre-planned, God-appointed and your name is written in the Lamb's Book of Life. Your salvation has come because of an obedient believer praying for you and releasing My Spirit for you unto salvation. It is also My desire and your responsibility to release My Spirit to other unsaved souls. It is My desire that everyone should be saved, so show no partiality. I send you into the world to save lost souls. Be My eyes, and be My ears and release My Spirit to each and every soul that you come in contact with. I will go where you ask Me to go."

July 22

Thus saith the Lord;

"I uphold the righteous. I turn My back and close My eye to the ungodly. The wicked will perish in their sins. Turn from your wicked ways; neither give place to the devil. Do not play with fire lest you get burnt. Continue in your walk with Me and mature in the spirit. Run the race like there is no tomorrow. The day draws nearer when the bridegroom will return. Be ready! Pray that you will be ready. Put the childish things behind you and be wise. Be careful because the time could come like a thief in the night. Rest assured, if you are in Me and I am in you then you will be ready."

July 23

Thus saith the Lord;

"My hand is mighty to save, to save you from the pit of hell, to save you from the snares of the enemy. I will shine My light upon you and you will be My shining light to a dark and perverse generation. Mighty things will be done in My name and for My kingdom. As My army grows stronger, the enemy's attacks will grow stronger. Do not fear. I have defeated the enemy on the cross and he will not prevail. The victory has been won. He is a defeated foe. Lift your eyes to heaven and say: 'My Lord, my God reigns on high from heaven above.'"

July 24

Thus saith the Lord;

"I honor your prayers and I answer them all. They are answered in a way that I see fit. It may not be in the way that you would hope or even expect. It could even seem to be a long time before you see the answer. My ways are higher than your ways. My thoughts are higher than your thoughts. Do not get discouraged. Answers to your prayers are coming. I am blessed everyday by your faithfulness."

July 25

Thus saith the Lord;

"I am breaking strongholds. I am breaking curses. I am breaking the chains and setting the captives free. I will deliver them from their enemies. My love I will pour out to them, for I am love. All power and authority has been given to Me. Nothing is too hard for Me. I am the Almighty. I hold the whole world in My hand and I am in control. My ways are incomprehensible to the natural man. I will give wisdom to whomever I please, but the gift of eternal life is free to anyone who asks. Ask and you shall receive."

July 26

Thus saith the Lord;

"Stand firm on the foundation of My Word. Do not sway. The enemy will come like a mighty storm to toss you to and fro, but My Word will not be shaken. That is why I say to stand strong on My Words. You will not be moved because your feet are planted on the rock. Do not believe the lies of the enemy. You believe in Me, believe in My Word and the things that I have already told you. Continue on the path that I have set before you. Continue to do the things that I have called you to do. My plans for you have not changed. You shall succeed, for if I am for you, who can be against you? Nothing is too hard for Me and I am in control. You have already begun to see My hand at work and it will continue. *Rejoice! Again, I say rejoice!"*

July 27

Thus saith the Lord;

"All things were created by Me, for Me, for My specific plan and purpose, for My pleasure and for My honor and glory. There is nothing that I cannot do and will not do for you. As a parent you would do anything to help your child, but often you have to step aside and let them suffer through many things so they can learn and grow. They learn and grow by their own experiences. I also allow you to learn and grow in the same way. There are many lessons to be learned. There are many things that I am teaching you. If you already knew all, then you would not need Me. Be an open vessel, be trainable, desire to learn, and desire to spend more time with Me. I desire to spend more time with you and I will teach you all things."

July 28

Thus saith the Lord;

"I am Love. You love Me because I first loved you. Love all those that I bring across your path. See your day as being led by Me. Everything that you see or do today has been pre-planned by Me. I am in control. When you start to understand and see that, then your whole attitude will change. You will have a new focus and it will be totally on Me. I go before you this day and prepare your way. I will lead the way."

July 29

Thus saith the Lord;

"Keep your eyes upon Me. No matter what your circumstances are, no matter what trials you are going through, no matter what is going on around you, stay focused on Me. I am all that matters. I am the one who loves you. I am the one taking care of you. I am the one in control. My plans are unfolding. I know that you cannot see it, but your faithfulness will be rewarded. Have faith. Have hope. Have love. The greatest of these is love. I am love. If you have love then you have Me."

July 30

Thus saith the Lord;

"There is a raging battle going on all around you, but do not fear. The battle belongs to me. I have already conquered death and the victory belongs to Me. It is a raging war for the souls. There are many lost souls and My army is marching forward. Release Me and My Spirit everywhere you go. My power lives in you and I give you authority to use My power. For without someone giving Me permission to move, I can do nothing. The more power you release the more power will come. It is My divine spiritual law."

July 31

Thus saith the Lord;

"Let the mighty river flow. I am the river and I want to flow through you, a constant flow, full of life, flourishing and nourishing many. All living things need water to survive. I am that water—the living water. I am sending many thirsty people across your path. You just need to give them a drink and point the way. Allow Me to flow through you and you will not thirst."

AUGUST

And all these blessings shall come upon you and overtake you,
because you obey the voice of the Lord your God

Deuteronomy 28:2

August 1

Thus saith the Lord;

"Just as certain that night and darkness will pass with the coming of dawn each new day, so will your troubles and problems pass too. For I hear your prayers. New doors will open and I will allow you to pass through. I am leading you down a road of new beginnings and great possibilities. I desire that you prosper. Everything that you put your hands to do, I will bless. I desire that your joy would be full. The joy of the Lord is contagious. It will spread to others. Do everything joyfully unto Me. You will be blessed."

August 2

Thus saith the Lord;

"I will heal the broken-hearted and bind up their wounds. I will turn what seems to be a hopeless situation into something wonderful and glorious. I will make the clouds disappear and the sun to brightly shine. I will mend that which is torn. I will repair that which is broken. I will restore that which has disintegrated. I will find that which is lost. I will replace that which is stolen. I will heal those who are sick. I will provide when there seems to be no provision. I will restore hope to the hopeless. Listen to Me! I say there is hope. I am the God of all hope! Put your hope and trust in Me."

August 3

Thus saith the Lord;

"This is a new day and yesterday will never come again. It is important to cherish every moment, be kind to every person, say the right thing, and do the right thing because you do not know what tomorrow will bring. Learn and live and grow in Me. Keep your eyes on Me. I am all you need. There is a veil over your eyes right now so that you cannot see Me. In heaven you will see Me and all My glory. Everything will be revealed to you in full. Right now it is only in part. Learn your lessons quickly so that this life will be easy. Believe and know that I am in control, you belong to Me, and I love you and am taking care of you."

August 4

Thus saith the Lord;

"Everything in the world can be shaken and destroyed, but I will not be shaken. My Word will endure forever. I am the All-Powerful, the Almighty, and the Everlasting God. Turn to Me and have everlasting peace, all hope, and eternal life so that you will be saved and spend eternity with Me. I have told you that all the works of the enemy shall be destroyed and that will come in many forms. Every force of nature heeds My command. I am in control of everything. Stay in My Word and you will not be shaken. The storms of life can rage all around you and you will be in perfect peace—a peace that only comes from Me."

August 5

Thus saith the Lord;

"Do not be as a frozen statue! Break forth into joy! Do you not understand what I have done for you? Do you not believe what I have given to you? You are not downcast. You will not be trodden under. You are a child of the King. Learn to live like a king's kid. Enjoy each day to the fullest. Not by might, not by power, but by My Spirit, saith the Lord. Expect great things. Everything is within your grasp; you only have to receive it. I am a giver and a rewarder of those who diligently seek Me. Be blessed My child, be blessed."

August 6

Thus saith the Lord;

"If you desire more of Me then you must give Me more of you. I am always here and I desire to spend time with you. I am never too busy and I will always come when you call. Just call on Me and I will be there. When you are lonely you can talk to Me. I will be your friend. When you are sad just talk to Me and I will comfort you. I am always here and I want to be with you all the time. I want to be all that you need."

August 7

Thus saith the Lord;

"If My Spirit lives in you, then you will bear much fruit. Be filled with the fruit of the Spirit. Desire all My gifts. Ask that you might receive them. Desire gifts and be ready to receive them. For when you ask and believe, then you shall receive. As the gifts are used they will multiply. When they are not used they will be taken away."

August 8

Thus saith the Lord;

"Drink of My water daily and you will never thirst. It is a spiritual river that will never run dry. Every life circumstance will be taken care of; every need will be met. I will do My part, but you must do your part. Stay in My Word; meditate on it day and night. Draw closer to Me and I will draw closer to you. Those who stay under My covering will be safe and no harm shall come to them. They will run and not grow weary. They will be blessed when they come in and blessed when they go out. They will be satisfied and when they lie down at night, they will have peaceful sleep. I am your Lord your God and you are My child—now be blessed."

August 9

Thus saith the Lord;

"Troubles will be all around you, but do not despair. Do not let them consume you. Rather, think of Me and all that I have done. Whatsoever things are lovely, whatsoever things are pure, think on these things. Give Me your burdens, problems, and cares of this world. Place them at My feet and allow Me to handle them and then you will have plenty of time to help Me. Life is short on this earth. Learn to trust Me more and more. I am your Father and I will take care of you and all those you love, for I love them too. Meditate on My Words day and night. Confess them with your mouth. Write them on your heart. They will be life to your soul and health to your bones. You will be victorious. Your soul will prosper. Now rejoice in your salvation, for your name is written in the Book of Life. Live! Live free of worry. Live for Me."

August 10

Thus saith the Lord;

"Watch for Me! Be ready and waiting for Me. I shall come and take you home to be with Me forevermore. The day draws near, but it is not time yet. Get your house in order. Prepare the way of the Lord. Be in My Word, be ready, and know what to look for. There are specific signs that I give to you. Only look unto Me. Do not be deceived by the world and the lusts therein. All you have to do is wait, watch, and be ready. Do not be afraid. It will be a glorious day when I return to take those home whom My Father has given to be with Me for all eternity. Rejoice! Again, I say rejoice that your name is written in the Lamb's Book of Life."

August 11

Thus saith the Lord;

"Exercise in the body profits the flesh. Exercise in the Lord profits the soul. Do not toil to become rich for you may waste many years and never obtain it, but rather toil in the Lord for he can make you rich. Everything you do, do it for the Lord. Your reward will come from Him. Do not seek approval from man. God sees all things and knows all things. He will supply all your needs according to His riches and glory in heaven. Thank the Lord for everything that you have."

August 12

Thus saith the Lord;

"I am the all-forgiving, compassionate Father—God. Confess your sins to Me and turn away from them, and I will help you abstain from them. You shall be washed as white as snow and be made new. The day is coming when sin will no longer have a place in your life. It will not plague you anymore. I will place a hedge of protection around you and the darts of the enemy will bounce off of it and will not touch you any longer. That day is coming. You must now resist the devil and he will flee from you. I will give you the strength to resist temptation. Be in My Word. Meditate on it day and night. The battle belongs to Me. Not by might—not by power—but by My Spirit, saith the Lord."

August 13

Thus saith the Lord;

"Desire My wisdom! Ask for My wisdom in all circumstances. A wise man will avoid the snares of the enemy. Wisdom is the beginning of Godliness. Seek it more than gold. Worldly possessions will perish, but the gifts I give will endure with you until the end. Therefore, humble yourself before Me, that I may exalt you in due time. The wise will walk in My council; they will not fear and will have plenty, because they did not waste or squander what was given to them by My Father. Know Me more. Wisdom and knowledge go hand-in-hand. Be wise in these last days!"

August 14

Thus saith the Lord;

"I know your heart and mind better than you know yourself. I know what you need even before you ask. Ask of Me anything in My name (*Jesus name*) and that is what I will do for you. Seek Me and My ways and your feet will follow My path. I will guide you by My eye. I see all and know all. I have many things for you to do for Me. I am compassionate and caring and all good things come from Me. You shall dwell safely in My loving arms and goodness and mercy shall follow you for the rest of your life. Let My love flow through you like a mighty river. Let My river flow."

August 15

Thus saith the Lord;

"My strength is made perfect in weakness. My grace is sufficient for you. I am all you need. Put your trust in Me. Do not worry; I have the whole world in My hands and I have a plan for your life. I am in control. When you ask Me to do something for you, believe that I will do it. You are My child and I am your loving Father in heaven—the Maker and Master of the universe and I care about you more than you can imagine. I formed you and made you in My image. You are My masterpiece. Live in My love and carry My love to others."

August 16

Thus saith the Lord;

"I will pour My Spirit out through you and will accomplish My plan and purpose for your life. You have yielded to Me and have given Me the right to live My life through you. It is not you who live, but it is I who live through you. Continue to yield to Me; you may rest, but I perform the work through you. It is My thoughts that I give to you—not yours. It is My wisdom that I give to you—not yours. It is My power that I give to you—not yours. I am conforming you into My image. Be willing, be able, be ready, and you will be used by Me."

August 17

Thus saith the Lord;

"My plans will unfold before your very eyes. Do not fear. Trust in Me only."

August 18

Thus saith the Lord;

"My ways are not your ways. You cannot know or see what I can. That is why I ask that you only trust in Me. Continue to pray for your loved ones. I will keep you in perfect peace when your mind is stayed upon Me. I am in control even when you think that I am not or when you think that I do not know what I am doing. I am doing a mighty work. Your life will be blessed and you will be exceedingly happy. Look backwards—you can see everything that I have done. You cannot see forward, but I can. I will never leave you nor forsake you. Resist the devil and he will flee from you. Stay in My Word and focus on Me. I am all that you need. Do not let the weight of the world burden you, but lift your burdens to Me and I will make your load lighter. I care for you and I love you. You will again see My hand at work. Trust Me."

August 19

Thus saith the Lord;

"I am not a God of punishment, but I am a re-warder of those who diligently seek Me. I am not a God of silence, but I commune with those that commune with Me. I am very compassionate, caring and loving. I continue to reach out and knock and am always trying to draw you closer to Me. I shall provide all that you need if you will let Me. I will do the work through you and give you rest if you will allow Me. You move and live and have your being because I have allowed it. Trust in Me! Without Me you have nothing. Look to Me for the answers. I will pour out My wisdom to you and give you the direction and the answers that you are seeking. I am the key to life. Yes, an abundant life. Live in Me and I will live in you."

August 20

Thus saith the Lord;

"You truly are not alone, for I am with you. Yes, you do not always see Me or feel Me, but I am here. Look for Me! You will see Me. You will see Me in the simple things. You will see Me in the beautiful things. Call My name and I will be there. I hear your every plea. Make time for Me. Talk with Me. I am always here and very near."

August 21

Thus saith the Lord;

"A life will not be measured by how much one has when they die, but rather how they have lived their life for Me. You have chosen to live your life with Me. Let Me live in you and through you. Die to yourself, for you have been bought with a price. You no longer belong to yourself, but you are mine. I will mold you and make you into My image. I love you just the way you are, and when I live through you then My righteousness will change your very character. You will love what I love; you will think about what I think about; you will hate what I hate. It will be My work to accomplish, not yours. You become like those you love. You are becoming more like Me every day."

August 22

Thus saith the Lord;

"Despite your situation, despite your circumstances you can receive an over whelming sense of peace and security from Me that can only come from Me. Rest in this peace; rest in this security. It comes from a sense of faith and trust in Me. You believe that I am in control. You trust in Me. It brings Me joy and pleasure knowing that your faith is increasing. Continue to grow. Continue to seek Me and My ways. My plans will unfold before your eyes. Even when you cannot see Me working—I am working. This is the faith that must continue. You need not know at all times: why? When? Where? Just trust Me. I am your Father and you are My child; believe in Me. I want only the best for My children. I love you. You are precious in My sight."

August 23

Thus saith the Lord;

"I want to be desired like a good habit—one that consumes your thought and mind. I don't want you to be able to live without Me, and I want to be in your thoughts the moment that you wake up in the morning. I want to be first and foremost in your life and in your thoughts all day long. Dedicate your life to Me. Dedicate your will to Me. Dedicate your love to Me. You will live satisfied and you will live with much joy and peace. This is My promise."

August 24

Thus saith the Lord;

"My joy can be your strength through every situation. You must take your eyes off yourself and your situation. Keep your heart, mind, and eyes on Me only. My strength is made perfect in your weakness. Let Me flow through you. Let Me work out the best solution to each of your problems. Give them to Me and let Me do the work. Dwell with Me. Live in My perfect peace. Acknowledge Me in all your ways and I will direct your path. My work will become evident in your life and My light will shine through you. Your light will draw many to Me. Rejoice for the glory of the Lord will come."

August 25

Thus saith the Lord;

"You question: 'what are you doing, Lord, in my life?' My work does not cease. I am constantly working on your behalf. I do not grow weary. I do not sleep. Just because you cannot see Me at work does not mean that I am not working. Please slow down; stop and commune with Me; pay attention because I am all around you; you just are not looking for Me. Spend time with Me and commune with Me just as you would with your child or spouse or parent. Those you love, you spend time with. Those you care about, you do things with. Those that you enjoy, you talk with. Those that you are compassionate about, you do things for. Spend time with Me and I will give you rest."

August 26

Thus saith the Lord;

"Die to yourself and let Me live through you. I will tell you what to do. I will tell you what to say. I will make My thoughts your thoughts. I will make you wise. I will live in you; no longer will it be you. I use the weak. I use the willing. I use the helpless. Let Me live in you so that My work can flow through you. I do not want you to do the work for Me. I want to be able to do My work through you. Be open to My flow. I will use My power to flow through you. Be open. Be My vessel."

August 27

Thus saith the Lord;

"Wait upon Me. Be still and know that I am God. Be patient and I will reveal My plans to you in due time. I am in control and I will point the way. You will know what to do when the time is right. My time is not your time. Until then, you must trust Me. Be happy and content knowing that I am working out a perfect plan. Take this time to learn and grow. Do those things that you know you should do and let Me do the rest. Right now I am calling you to pray."

August 28

Thus saith the Lord;

"The rain that I am pouring out across the land represents the blessings that I will pour out to all people in these last days. Do not be deceived! It is the beginning of many sorrows. The blessings will be short lived. Do not squander what I give you, but rather be as the wise servant. Spend wisely and store up food for the coming days. I shall take care of those who heed My voice. I prepared Noah and his family for the flood. I will prepare you and your family for what lies ahead. Do not worry. Just get ready."

August 29

Thus saith the Lord;

"Pain and suffering should not be viewed as punishment, but rather as strengthening and growth in one's life. Learn to lean on My everlasting arms. I will heal your heart and bind up your wounds. There is nothing that I would not do for you. More of Me will mean less of you. Die to yourself and let Me live through you. I will turn your sorrow into joy. I will turn your pain into relief and your suffering into glory-filled praise. Rejoice, My child! Rejoice! I am the King of Glory and I am alive. I can make that which is dead alive again. I can make the blind to see and the deaf to hear. I will restore to you what the canker worm has eaten, for I am the God of restoration. Be patient and trust Me."

August 30

Thus saith the Lord;

"Your praise and worship are as sweet incense. It brings Me great pleasure and I am honored. I will pour out more of myself to you. I will pour out more of myself to My church which is My body. My power will be revealed. My strength will pour out to My people. My glory will shine through the veil. My love will overflow. Signs and wonders and miracles will be performed. Not by might, not by power, but by My Spirit, saith the Lord."

August 31

Thus saith the Lord;

"This day you will see My hand at work. Look for it constantly—all day. I will reveal Myself to you in a new way. I am doing a new thing, a mighty thing. You ask and you shall receive. Be blessed My child. Receive all that I have for you."

SEPTEMBER

Casting down arguments and every high thing that exalts itself
against the knowledge of God, bringing every thought into
captivity to the obedience of Christ

2 Corinthians 10:5

September 1

Thus saith the Lord;

"Don't give up. Continue to pray. You will see a breakthrough. Your prayers are being answered. Discouragement is not from Me. Failure is not from Me. Cast down vain imaginations. I have not left you. Look upward and say, 'all is well, my Lord is in control.'"

September 2

Thus saith the Lord;

"My hand is not too short that it cannot save. For My saving grace is for all, but not all will receive it."

September 3

Thus saith the Lord;

"Do not worry about your finances. Everything that you have has come from My hand. I have the ability to give or take, for all is in My control. Be thankful for what you have. Give and it shall be given to you. That is My spiritual law. Do not be anxious for anything, but by prayer and supplication, let your requests be made known to Me. I will take care of you, for I love you."

September 4

Thus saith the Lord;

"My precious child, I am always here. I know your heart and needs better than you know yourself. Do not fret or worry. You are special in My sight. I know your struggles. I know your short comings. Lean not to your own understanding, but acknowledge Me in all your ways and I will direct your paths. I love you more than you can comprehend. I want you to be happy and live in My flow. Learn to live in My power and let Me live through you."

September 5

Thus saith the Lord;

"Those things that you confess with your mouth and believe in your heart shall surely come to pass. Confess My Words and My promises over your house, your family, your finances, your health, and over all that concerns you. Confess them daily, weekly, and monthly, and they will come to pass. For My Words do not return unto Me void. They are life to your bones and health to your flesh. What I have spoken already belongs to you, but you must accept it."

September 6

Thus saith the Lord;

"It brings Me great pleasure to hear My children pray. It brings Me joy when you are joyful. It makes Me smile when you smile. I feel all that you feel. All that you seek, you shall find—for when you seek, you shall find. I desire that you be in good health and prosper even as your soul prospers. You shall obtain that. Let My Words dwell richly in your heart and mind. I have so much to give you. I can hardly restrain the blessings that await you. You must prepare yourself to receive. I only reveal to you what you are ready for. Continue in Me. Continue in prayer. Continue in My Word."

September 7

Thus saith the Lord;

"My hand is upon you and all that you do. My Words shall be established in your heart, and they shall endure forever. When anyone asks anything of you, give it to them. Give to those in need. Help those who are less fortunate than you. You must learn the laws of giving. Ask Me to show you someone in need, and then do your part and give. You will be blessed."

September 8

Thus saith the Lord;

"I have not come to condemn the world, but to give life and life more abundantly. Let Me give to you this life. Live the life of joy and peace. Live it with Me, each day, for I am the bread of life. The closer you are to Me the more imperfect you will feel. This is not bad, it is good. I have asked you to be perfect just as I am perfect; however you will not obtain perfection in this life. It is necessary to strive for it. Someday you will be made perfect. Each new day, in union with Me, be a little stronger, a little better, and a little kinder in some way. Again, I say to you that I do not look at your failures just your possibilities. I look at your progress. I love you and you are mine."

September 9

Thus saith the Lord;

"You must trust Me with your whole heart and lean not to your own understanding; acknowledge Me in all your ways and I will direct your paths. Hold on to the things that I have told you because they will come to pass. You cannot change the plans that I have for you. I need you more than you need Me. Look at the past. Have I not worked out all your other problems? Give all of your problems to Me. I have much in store for you and you will rejoice."

September 10

Thus saith the Lord;

"There is nothing that I cannot do. All things are possible with Me. There is nothing too big or too small. Give them all to Me. It is My great pleasure to give you My kingdom. I do love to see you happy. I love the times we share together. Please, My child, do not fret or worry. I truly am in control of your life. Let Me prove Myself, tomorrow and the rest of today—no more worries. Just say, 'My Lord, My Savior will handle this.'"

September 11

Thus saith the Lord;

"Do not be attached to the things of the world. They are temporal. Rather, store up your treasures in heaven, for they are eternal. No stone shall be left unturned means that I will expose all hidden things in the lives of those whom I have called. Remember, I have chosen you. You have not chosen Me. I am perfecting that which I love and have made. You cannot run nor hide. I am gentle and kind. I love you and you are My child. Just as you rear your children, guiding them and teaching them right from wrong, I too am guiding you and teaching you. It is not hard! I am helping you."

September 12

Thus saith the Lord;

"Stand strong. Fight the good fight of faith. I have given you the weapons to battle the enemy. Your feet are planted on the rock. You feel like you are losing control, but you can't because I, your Maker, am in control. Greet each day with new vitality, renewed hope, and expectation because I, the Lord God Jehovah am doing mighty things. I am coming in might and power. The changes you are praying for and desiring will come to pass."

September 13

Thus saith the Lord;

"Do not fear. Many things will come to pass. My kingdom will not be shaken, but other kingdoms will fall. Many will turn against Me saying I am to blame. They will be blinded by the powers of the enemy for a time. Do not drift to the right or to the left, but stay on the path laid before you. I will not leave you desolate. My power will rise within you. You will be My beloved bride and I your groom. The hearts of men and woman will be divided—some who are lukewarm and cold will turn colder. Others who are lukewarm and hot will catch on fire and will serve Me with their whole heart, their whole mind, and will trust only Me. They will endure and abide with Me forever."

September 14

Thus saith the Lord;

"Be free of the negative thoughts, worries, and troubles that consume you. I want to occupy your thoughts. I want to be all that you think about. I want to be the love of your life. When you achieve that goal, all else will fall into place. I am all that you need. I know you better than anyone, for I made you. I know your thoughts. I know your heart and mind. I will not disappoint you. I will provide your every need. I love you and will be with you every step of the way. I will never leave you."

September 15

Thus saith the Lord;

"Be kind and loving and caring to one another. You are doing work for Me. Be a helping hand, a listening ear, or say a kind word. Whatever you do, if you do it unto Me, you will be doing work for Me. Work for Me and My kingdom. Whatsoever you sow, you shall reap. Whatever seed that you plant I will water and nourish. Labor in love and labor for Me."

September 16

Thus saith the Lord;

"I desire to be needed and loved by you. I want to be the love of your life. Are you willing to give up everything to follow Me? I want to be all that you need. Commune with Me and I will commune with you. Seek Me with your whole heart and I will reveal many mighty things to you. Godly wisdom will I give to you and keys to unlock the mysteries of My kingdom. Strife and struggles will cease. Life will be easier as you learn to live in Me and let Me flow through you.

Live in My peace, in My joy, and in My love. Goodness and mercy shall follow you all the days of your life. Rejoice!"

September 17

Thus saith the Lord;

"My children's gifts will increase. Others will receive strong delusions. My ways will be made known to many. Others will veer off My path. My sheep know My voice. Others follow strange voices. Make no mistake. Not all will come to know Me. The stage for the battlefield is taking place. The war for the souls has begun."

September 18

Thus saith the Lord;

"I bring people across your path that need Me—help them to find Me. Point the way. Drop seeds. Pray for them. For what you do to others you also do to Me."

September 19

Thus saith the Lord;

"Your eyes will behold My coming. It shall be in this generation. Be ready and watching, for it will be a glorious uniting—the groom to his bride. For this reason you should rejoice. Upon My return—no more sorrow—no more fear—no more tears—no more pain. This is your hope. Be strong and patient and wait upon the Lord."

September 20

Thus saith the Lord;

"Have no fear. For I have not given you the spirit of fear, but of power and love and a sound mind. Those who love Me shall have My peace and My rest. Despite all the evil you see, you shall see much more good. My blessings will abound and My provisions will be abundant. Keep your eyes on Me only, for all other things will bring you down. Your sleep will be sweet and your mouth shall be satisfied. The world will see My power and My glory come."

September 21

Thus saith the Lord;

"My delight is in you—watching you grow—watching you live. Be anxious for nothing. I am in control and all is from My hand. You will not lack any good thing. Trust in Me. Walk with Me; commune with Me. You were made for Me. Love Me and live for Me. I am all you need."

September 22

Thus saith the Lord;

"Your ways are not My ways. Your thoughts are not My thoughts. Give all to Me, for I know all and I see all. I know the beginning to the end. You only see in part and know in part. You must keep your eyes on Me: upward, heavenwards so you won't be misled, confused, or depressed. The world and those who are without Me shall be torn apart and tormented by the evil one. Do not see the way the world sees, but see without your eyes: see in faith."

September 23

Thus saith the Lord;

"My path is not always easy or straight, but rest assured that I am leading the way. I am with you always, and I will never leave you nor forsake you. I am in control. Your circumstances are not by chance. No, they are not a mistake. I am molding you and making you into My image. *Be changeable!* Desire change in your life. Do not be content to continue the same way in your life. *Desire more!* Desire all that I have for you. Do not settle for second best. *Seek Me! Seek*

My ways! The best is yet to come. I have much in store for you. I desire that you be in good health and that you prosper. Goodness and mercy shall follow you the rest of your life. You will be blessed in your comings and goings. No harm shall come to you. You will dwell safely and have great peace. I love you My child; you belong to Me."

September 24

Thus saith the Lord;

"The closer you get to Me, the closer I am to you. The more you commune with Me, the more I commune with you. The more you love others, the more you will be loved. The more you give away, the more you will receive. It is My spiritual law. It is contrary to the world's ways. You are My child in whom I am well pleased. Continue on My path that I have put before you. You will do many mighty works in My name for My kingdom. A new faith will arise within your spirit. There will be nothing that you cannot do in the power of *Jesus'* name. Use My name often. There is power in the name of *Jesus* and in the blood of *Jesus*. In *Jesus* name, be made whole!"

September 25

Thus saith the Lord;

"My plans are unfolding for your life. Seek Me and My ways, and My plans will become more apparent. My plans to prosper and use you will unfold. Your love for Me grows stronger. Your faith in Me increases. Your relationship with Me grows deeper. No good thing will I withhold from you. You shall begin to reap what you have sown. You shall abound in blessings. Rejoice, My child, rejoice and be exceedingly glad."

September 26

Thus saith the Lord;

"Do not fear. I am working out the best possible plan for your life. My provisions are abundant."

September 27

Thus saith the Lord;

"You shall see My goodness and My mercy. I love My people. Those who love Me shall see: I am in control; I am a rewarder of those who diligently seek Me; I am just, and I am coming again. You must remember when you are weak—I am strong. I have the power to change the course of the world. I can change your circumstances. Have faith and trust. I am doing good things for you. They are for the ones I love. I love you. Stay close to Me and I will stay close to you."

September 28

Thus saith the Lord;

"A day does not go by when I do not think of you. A day does not go by that I do not love you. I constantly care for you. My provisions are never ending. My grace is sufficient. My forgiveness is endless. My compassion is great. My understanding is infinite. My child, do not fret or worry, for I am in control, and I will take care of you. Let your faith grow. Let your trust deepen. Let your love widen. Grow closer to Me, and I will grow closer to you. You are safe with Me, and I shall guide you by My eye. My hands are upon you and you have My blessings. Rejoice."

September 29

Thus saith the Lord;

"My blessings flow to the world. I especially want to bless those who believe in Me. I want to bless those who believe that I am a rewarder of those who diligently seek Me. Seek Me with your whole heart, your whole mind, and your whole soul, and you will abide satisfied. I am He who has come to save the world. I love you and I know that you love Me. Ask Me for those things that you need, those things that you desire, and those things that you want. I will supply all your needs according to My riches and glory in heaven. If you do not ask, you shall not receive. Many lack because they have not asked. I desire that My glory fill your life while you live on the earth. Be blessed this day and every day for the rest of your life."

September 30

Thus saith the Lord;

"I not only want you to be a giver, but I want you to be able to receive also. There are many things that I want to give to you. Be open and be willing. Believe that you receive what you ask for before you see it, by confessing it with your mouth. Confess it. Give praise and thanks for it. Confess My Word out loud with your mouth. 'Thank you, God, that you heal all of My diseases according to your Word. By *Jesus'* stripes I am healed. Thank you *Jesus*, that I am healed.' The spoken Word is powerful. Use it daily. Say it until you believe it. Confess it, believe it, expect it, and it will come to pass. You must receive by faith."

OCTOBER

And God will wipe away every tear from their eyes; there shall be no more death, nor sorrow, nor crying. There shall be no more pain, for the former things have passed away.

Revelation 21:4

October 1

Thus saith the Lord;

"My kingdom will be glorious. It will be where all mankind will be united as one, sharing the same Spirit, worshipping the one and only God. It will be all joy and no sorrow—no more pain or suffering—just radiant souls basking in the Savior's love for them. There will be beautiful music in heaven. All will be clothed in His righteousness. We will all see His glory and be able to look right into His face and loving eyes. At that time, we will understand it all, because everything will be revealed to us. What a glorious day that will be."

October 2

Thus saith the Lord;

"This day nothing will come your way that you cannot handle. I am with you and I have equipped you with all the necessary tools. Lean on Me. When you are weak, I am strong. Say, 'I can do all things through Christ who strengthens me.' Be patient, as I am patient with you telling you the same things over and over again. You must hear these things often until they permeate your mind and become reality in your life. Please be patient with your loved ones, just as I am patient with you. Treat them as you want Me to treat you. Let My love flow through you. You are pointing the way toward Me and My kingdom. I love you and I go before you to prepare your way. Be blessed, My child."

October 3

Thus saith the Lord;

"I know your heart and thoughts. They are good and not evil. I do not condemn you when you sin. I would rather that you made a mistake to learn and grow as a result, than to stay in the same place. Most of life's lessons are learned by experiences. The same is true spiritually. If everything were easy for you, how well would you know Me? How much would you trust Me? How much would you love Me? He who loves Me little has been forgiven little; he who loves Me a lot has been forgiven a lot. There is a purpose and a reason for everything. It is My purpose and My reason. Know that I love you."

October 4

Thus saith the Lord;

"I freely give to you and I want you to freely give to others. Give without expectation of receiving. Your reward will come from Me, for all things come from Me. Let Me overflow and spill like a new wine from a new flask. Let others drink the excess, for you are My chosen vessel among a dying world. You are to help point the way to Me. I am the way, the life, and the truth. No man comes to the Father except, through Me, *Jesus* Christ. Say, '*Jesus*, come into My life,' and I will give you eternal life. Ask so your sins may be forgiven, and I will wash you as white as snow. I will fill you with new wine which is My Holy Spirit."

October 5

Thus saith the Lord;

"You will have trials and tribulations in your life and in the world, but be of good cheer, for I have overcome the world. They do not come as a punishment, but rather as a purifying process. Welcome changes in your life. Welcome My Holy Spirit in your life. I have come that you may have a more abundant life. Let Me lead you to this abundant life. I am all that you need. There is nothing that I cannot do. Live for Me and I will live in you. I give My angels charge over you. Soon My blessings will consume you and overtake you, and you will not have room to receive them all. You will have to give some of them away. Be ready to be blessed and to be a blessing to others."

October 6

Thus saith the Lord;

"You are a new creation. Once you have asked for My forgiveness and asked Me into your heart you will be made new. You no longer live, but I live in you. You are precious in My sight and you belong to Me. I will accomplish in you the good work that I have begun. Let My Words dwell richly in your heart. They are transforming, life changing, and they will alter your thoughts and renew your mind. They are health and life to your bones. Stay in My Word every day to keep the doctor away. Be not conformed to the world, for the world and the lusts of the world will pass away, but My Words shall endure forever."

October 7

Thus saith the Lord;

"All good and perfect things come from your Father in heaven. Seek Me and My kingdom and all these things will be added to you. Not a day goes by that My thoughts are not on you. I love you and I desire that you prosper and be in good health. Let My light shine to the world. Be a lighthouse for My glory and My power. I will use you to touch many people for My kingdom. Be willing. Be useable. Hearken unto My voice and I will tell you what to do. With Me, all things are possible to those who believe. All you have to do is believe. The rest is up to Me."

October 8

Thus saith the Lord;

"Sorrow may endure for the night, but joy will come in the morning. Stay in My Word and draw closer to Me in your sad times. I will comfort you. Lift your cares and concerns to Me. I can take your burdens and make your load lighter. Trust in Me with your whole heart and lean not on your own understanding. It is not necessary that you know what I am doing. Just believe that when you give

Me something to handle, I will accomplish what I desire to do. Trust in Me. Have the trust of a child. Have a child-like faith. The enemy would have you worry and fret over every little thing. Worry is produced by a lack of trust. Do not worry, for worry does not accomplish any good thing. Trust in Me only. Trust Me, I say."

October 9

Thus saith the Lord;

"To each man was given the freedom of choice. It is your God-given right to choose whom you may serve. To each I give a measure of faith. You must choose to cultivate it. My gifts are freely given to anyone who asks, but they cost Me dearly. I gave My beloved son that you might have life—a more abundant life. I do not show partiality. I love each the same. My delight is in My children. All is within your power and reach. Speak blessings and not curses. Choose to love. Choose to forgive. Choose to serve. Choose to live your life with Me."

October 10

Thus saith the Lord;

"I love the times that we spend together. I look forward to the conversations that we have. I want to hear from you as much as you want to hear from Me. Converse with Me as you would a best friend. I am available at all times. I am never too busy for you, and I can be all you need. Whatever you need, I can meet that need. I cherish our love and I will never leave you. I will be with you forever, because you will be with Me in heaven for all eternity."

October 11

Thus saith the Lord;

"I am very concerned about you and all that you do. I know the number of hairs on your head. I hear your every cry. I hear your every plea. My plans for you are beyond your comprehension. Please do not worry. You must grasp My power and the infinite wisdom I have; I am in control. Look for My hand at work all around you. Seek My help in all of your affairs. Let Me rule in your heart and mind. Be anxious for nothing, but by prayer and supplication, let your requests be made known to Me. My peace I give unto you. Let My peace rule in your heart and mind; My perfect peace casts out all fear."

October 12

Thus saith the Lord;

"Happy is the man who puts his trust in the Lord. He shall abide satisfied. He will lie down at night and have peaceful sleep. He will be the head and not the tail. He will be blessed when he comes in and blessed when he goes out. The Lord will make his way prosperous, and he will see much fruit from his labor. The Lord will make His face to shine upon him and find great favor in him. Do not strive to be successful; rather strive for the Lord, and He will make you successful. Blessed be the name of the Lord. Bless His holy name."

October 13

Thus saith the Lord;

"My mercies are never ending. My promises are true. My love shall endure forever. Prepare yourself for heaven, because that is where you will spend eternity with Me. I have gone before you to prepare a place for you. Get a heaven mindset and you will be less attached to the world and the lusts therein. Where your heart is, your mind will be also. This is the day that I have made, rejoice and be glad in it. It is your choice and within your power to make this the best day ever. My peace is in you and My joy is in you. Be determined to live in peace and joy. I love you and you belong to Me. Together, we can make a difference."

October 14

Thus saith the Lord;

"There are hidden treasures in My Word. Seek them out as if they were gold. Confess out loud My promises and blessings, for the spoken Word stirs the spirit. It was by your confession that you were saved. You were not saved by your works or deeds. There is creative power in My spoken Word. My spoken name has power. My spoken Word is sharper than a two-edged sword. Learn My Words. Learn to speak them. You will be able to call those things that are not yet as though they were. This will happen because you believe in Me and My power and know that My ways are contrary to the world's ways. This is the faith that I want you to have."

October 15

Thus saith the Lord;

"Blessed are the peacekeepers, for they shall inherit the kingdom of God. Blessed are they that seek after righteousness, for they will see God. Blessed are those who keep My commandments, for they will inherit eternal life. Blessed are those who forgive, for they will be forgiven. Blessed are those who feed the hungry, for they will be fed. Blessed are those who will be ready and watching. Blessed are those who will hear the trumpet. Blessed are those who will see the Lord ascend from the heavens. Blessed are those who will go to meet the Lord face to face. Stay sober, be diligent, and stay in My Word. You do not know the day or the hour that I will come to get you. **Be ready!**"

October 16

Thus saith the Lord;

"Bless the Lord with all of your heart, your mind, your soul, and with all of your strength. Bless the Lord with all that is within you. Bless His Holy name. The whole earth is filled with His glory. Blessings, honor, and glory belong to the Lord. He is worthy of your praise.

Magnify and exalt Him this day. Let everything that has breath, praise His holy name."

I will proclaim the name of the Lord. Oh, praise the greatness of our God! (Deuteronomy 32:3)

October 17

Thus saith the Lord;

"Be bold in your faith! Be confident and know who you are! You are a child of God: the King of Kings, the Author and Finisher of your faith, the Alpha and the Omega. I am unstoppable. I am unmovable. I am in control. My will for you has not changed and it will come to pass. Enjoy My blessings, for they are many, and My mercies are new every day. Do not fear what the future may hold, for I am in control, and I will take care of you."

October 18

Thus saith the Lord;

"Whatsoever things are praise-worthy; whatsoever things are lovely; whatsoever things are honest and true; think on these things, for as a man thinks in his heart, his actions will surely reveal his heart. Delight yourself in the Lord and He will give you the desires of your heart. All good and perfect gifts come from My Father in heaven. You are My gift from My Father. You have been wondrously made. My delight is in you."

October 19

Thus saith the Lord;

"Thank Me for your hurts, your pains, your struggles, your lack, your weaknesses, and all trials and tribulations. For without them, you would not need Me. A well person does not need a physician. The times that you drift away from Me are the times that you are doing the best physically and mentally, but not necessarily spiritually. The times you need Me the most are when you are the worst physically and mentally, but you are often more spiritually attuned to Me. My child, learn to live each day with Me as you would with a loved one. I change not, and My arms are always open wide. I love you."

October 20

Thus saith the Lord;

"Not all things are bad. I can turn what seems to be a bad situation into something wonderful and beautiful; it is through My miracle-working power. Hearts must be tried and tested, like a refining process. The outcome will be better than the beginning. Please know that whatever you are going through, I am there with you and you must surrender to Me, so I can work out the most glorious outcome for your situation. It will be My way, My plan for you, even if the trial was because of your own mistakes. Repent and be forgiven. Learn from your mistakes, grow stronger, grow wiser and live. Learn to live in Me and have freedom from guilt and worry. I will show you the way."

October 21

Thus saith the Lord;

"Good things come to those who wait. Wait upon the Lord. He will renew you and give you wings like eagles to mount and fly. Fly high above your situation, and soar above any problem. Remember, I am there with you in the midst of it all. No harm shall come to a single hair on your head. You will run and not grow weary. You will not faint. My angels I give charge over you. The enemy cannot harm you. My peace I give to you—everlasting peace. Stay close to Me. Sing, praise, and worship Me, and the devil will flee from you. His temptations will cease. He is a defeated foe. There is nothing he can do to snatch you from Me. You belong to Me. Rejoice. Rejoice that you will spend eternity with Me."

October 22

Thus saith the Lord;

"Do not grow weary in well-doing, for in due time you shall reap. The enemy comes in like a flood to kill, steal, and destroy. But I am mightier than he. The victory is mine, saith the Lord. I give you your life; I hold you with My mighty hands; I give you power to tread over the enemy, for I am the great I Am. Stand firm, for your feet are planted upon the rock, and when the flood recedes, your house will surely stand. I shall accomplish all that I said that I would accomplish, and you will reign with Me forevermore. I am your God and you are My child. I love you."

October 23

Thus saith the Lord;

"Continue to walk in the way that you are going because your steps are ordered by Me. I go before you and lead the way. Do not worry, for I am in control. Acknowledge Me in all things and I will direct your paths. There is a light at the end of the tunnel and you will rejoice. Remember, as I have said before, some of these times are growth periods. When you feel like you can stand no more—I say to you: stand, be strong and of good courage. Pray—cease not to pray. Look to others, for when you are weak, they are strong. Again, I say to you that two are better than one."

October 24

Thus saith the Lord;

"Do you know how much I love you? I love you so much that I gave My only begotten son so that you would not perish, but have ever-lasting life. Dwell on these things. Your problems are like giants in your life because you have allowed them to rule your life. Dwell on My love for you, the things I have already done for you, and what I am about to do for you. I am working out the best possible plan for your life. Cast down doubt, worry, sickness, poverty, and everything that is not of Me. I will supply your needs."

October 25

Thus saith the Lord;

"Be less concerned about yourself and more concerned about those around you. Be not conformed to the world, but be conformed to My Word. Live in the Spirit, live for the Spirit and become as the Spirit. As you draw closer to Me, I will draw closer to you. It will be as if scales are removed from your eyes. I will bring you to a new spiritual level and you will be able to see more clearly. Sing, praise, and worship, for all of these will bring you into My presence. It is good to be in My presence."

October 26

Thus saith the Lord;

"There is so much work to be done. I need willing hearts and serving hands. My kingdom is bountiful. I have so much to offer to all that will come. Come to Me all you who labor and I will give you rest. My grace is sufficient and My yoke is light."

October 27

Thus saith the Lord;

"Don't worry about the things to come. They are in My hand and in My power. Remember things are not always as they may appear. I have abundant blessings in store for you. I am deeply moved by your situation. My peace I give to you. I will give you everlasting peace and abundant joy. Your loved ones must come to Me and I will restore them also. Abide in Me and I will abide in you. I love you."

October 28

Thus saith the Lord;

"Your footsteps are ordered by the Lord. Where I lead, you will follow. Do not fear what tomorrow may bring. My tender mercies are new every day."

October 29

Thus saith the Lord;

"Be still! Be still, My child, and know that I am God. I am your Lord, your Maker, and Creator of all things. *Stop your quarreling! Stop your fretting!* All power has been given to Me. I can help you—only I—not your brother, not your mother, not your lawyer. Come unto Me. Tell Me the problems, the worries, the cares and then leave them with Me. I will make your load lighter. I will answer your prayers and give you solutions to your problems. It is My great privilege to not only help you, but to be your friend also. I love you. You must trust Me."

October 30

Thus saith the Lord;

"He who abides in Me shall be satisfied and I shall keep him in perfect peace whose mind is stayed upon Me. Do not let your mind rule your heart, but rather let your heart rule your mind. The mind is carnal. The heart is spiritual. I reign and live in your heart. The mind is a battlefield for the enemy. Again, I say do not let the mind rule your heart, but rather let the heart rule your mind. This sounds simple, but it is not so. Reflect on this truth and your mind will obey your heart. For out of your heart flows the springs of life."

October 31

Thus saith the Lord;

"Pray for your enemies. Pray for those who hurt you and despitefully use you. Do not kick a man when he is down, but rather help him up. Do not put blame on others. Consider yourself and try to improve yourself. Make peace with one another for you do not know what tomorrow may hold. Be kind, love, and be patient. For your reward will come from Me."

NOVEMBER

And let the peace of God rule in your hearts, to which also you were called in one body; and be thankful. Let the Word of Christ dwell in you richly in all wisdom, teaching and admonishing one another in psalms and hymns and spiritual songs, singing with grace in your hearts to the Lord. And whatever you do in word or deed, do all in the name of the Lord *Jesus*, giving thanks to God the Father through Him.

Colossians 3:15-17

November 1

Thus saith the Lord;

"I am a compassionate God. I am caring and full of love. My love is perfect. I am all that you need. My love will permeate out of your being. My joy will radiate out of your spirit. My peace will rule in your heart. My wisdom will fill your head and mind. Rejoice My child and be exceedingly glad. I am your God and you are My beloved child."

November 2

Thus saith the Lord;

"No, joy is not a commandment of mine. It is your choice; so are many of your actions and emotions, some of which may quench My Spirit working in you. Do not despair. I will never leave you nor forsake you. Look to Me, call on Me and I will lift you up. Remember to dwell on the good things that I have done."

November 3

Thus saith the Lord;

"You feel like the walls are crumbling down around you, like your building is being destroyed by an earthquake. Everything around you is being shaken. Your feet are planted on a rock. No harm shall come to you. All other things are temporal, but your spirit will live with Me for all eternity. Do not be afraid, for I am in control. Keep your eyes focused on Me. I will keep you in perfect peace through the storm. I will deliver you from destruction. Do not despair. Continue in My Word and in Me. The enemy cannot take what I have given to you. He is a defeated foe. *Look up, and see me in all my glory!* You belong to Me and I love you."

November 4

Thus saith the Lord;

"Continue to let My light shine. Oh, how I love you. You shall prosper. The day is coming when money will no longer be a worry for you. Trust in Me. I will take care of you. You are a delight to Me as you are to others. You are faithful. You shall be blessed."

November 5

Thus saith the Lord;

"Those around you are drawn to you by My Spirit. People are attracted to light, and as a child of God you possess My light. It is My Spirit. Many are drawn to My kingdom by watching Spirit-filled lives. You are My witness to a lost and dying world. Pray for those I send across your path, for when my children ask, that moves my Father's heart to move on their behalf. Yes, I know all and see all, but you must ask what you will before I will answer. I am not a forceful God, but all power is in My hand. I am a loving God, but I wait for you to ask for my help. Be sensitive to the needs of others and lift them to Me, thus allowing My Spirit to move and help. Let your light shine to a lost and dying world. I love you."

November 6

Thus saith the Lord;

"There is not one person who I do not love. Even so, you too should love everyone. For this is one of My great commandments: love your neighbor as yourself. First you must love Me. Then My love will empower you to love yourself and others."

November 7

Thus saith the Lord;

"You are chosen. You are where you are today because I have placed you there. Your life is what it is today because I have chosen it for you. I have plans for you. They entail your life today. Seek My plans. I will use you to do My work. Do not think that you are nothing because you are everything to Me. I gave My life for you. I will use every little bit of yourself that you give to Me, so surrender yourself to Me."

November 8

Thus saith the Lord;

"Stay in My Word. Stand on My promises. Know that I am faithful to those who are mine. I care for the birds in the air and the flowers in the field. You are more valuable to Me than the birds and the flowers. Trust Me. Believe Me. Love Me. These are strong qualities. The enemy cannot prevail against these. Rise up and be strong, for the Lord God Almighty is in you. Know that I am God and know My power. When this revelation becomes reality in your heart and mind, your life will change."

November 9

Thus saith the Lord;

"You must know that I am working—working to bring about changes—changes for your good and My glory. Do not be sad. Do not worry. I am in control. I love you. You are My beloved child, in whom I am well-pleased. Think of these rough times—these tough times—as quality time with Me. They are training times, strengthening times, and times of refreshing. They are times to bring about good, to bring about change. They are needed times. Can you not see this? Pray for My will to be done. I am working. I am working. During the storm you cannot see clearly. It is not until the storm is passed that you can see. You are not alone, for I go before you. Follow Me."

November 10

Thus saith the Lord;

"Those that belong to Me, I will take care of. I will guide them by My eye. I will cover them with the shadow of My wings. No harm shall come near their dwelling. They shall pray to Me and I will hear them. I love them and they love Me. This is My promise to them."

November 11

Thus saith the Lord;

"Do not give up the good fight of faith. Continue to fight, be strong, and of good courage. I am with you and I am for you. If I am for you, who can be against you? You are under My shield. You are under My control. You are under My protection. I am in control. The very thought of My name should bring you peace. The very thought of My love should bring you love. The very thought of My strength should bring you strength. The very thought of My power should bring you power. I am the way, the life, and the truth. If you have Me, then indeed you have these."

November 12

Thus saith the Lord;

"Rejoice and fret not. Let Me have My way in your life. I will accomplish in you a mighty work—free from worry and care—one of love and luxury in Me. I will lead you beside the running water in the valley of plenty and goodness; goodness and mercy will follow you the rest of your life. Fear will be far from you. My light in you will shine as bright as the noon day."

November 13

Thus saith the Lord;

"Do not judge one another, for with the measure you judge, you will be judged. Forgive one another's faults, for there is none perfect and without sin except Me. Ask for your sins to be revealed to you, so that you may turn from them and look to Me. I will help you and deliver you when you seek My forgiveness and My help. Do not esteem yourself better than another, for I love you all just the same. Love one another as I have loved you."

November 14

Thus saith the Lord;

"I shall open My window from heaven and pour out My blessings to you. Mighty blessings shall flow. You will not have room for all of My blessings. Pass My blessings onto others. I will bring people across your path that I want you to bless. The more you give away; the more blessings you will receive; it is My spiritual law. Give and it will be given to you. I will tell you what to give, when to give, and to whom to give. Listen to My voice. Be not afraid, for it is not by might, not by power, but by the Almighty God through whom all blessings flow. Like a flowing mighty river, I will pour out blessings to you. Be glad. Be exceedingly glad. Live in My Spirit. Breathe in My Spirit. *Jesus* is a name that you can trust. Say My name often. '*Jesus, Jesus, Jesus.*'"

November 15

Thus saith the Lord;

"Learn to live each day to the fullest. Relax in Me and have joy in Me. Trust in Me with your whole heart and believe that I am in control. Lift your stress and problems to Me and I will handle them. Then you will be free to laugh and love more. This is the kind of day that I desire for you. There is nothing that can come your way today that

I cannot handle. When you learn to let Me help you, every day will truly be a nice day."

November 16

Thus saith the Lord;

"Today, nothing will come your way that I cannot handle. Give all your cares and concerns to Me. I will take care of you. I love you and you are wondrously made. This is the day that I have made, be glad and rejoice in it."

November 17

Thus saith the Lord;

"I am a loving and just God. Put your faith wholly and totally in Me. Believe that I care for you and watch over you. Trust in Me. I have a perfect plan for your life that I am working out in the best possible way. Your loved ones are in My care."

Prayer:

God, I will try to trust in you with my whole heart and know that what you are doing is for my own good. I believe that you will move good people into my life and others out of my life who does not serve your purposes for me. I will try not to lean on my own understanding, but I believe you are accomplishing your will in my life for my own good and for your honor and glory. Help Me Lord. This is what I want.

November 18

Thus saith the Lord;

"I am a forgiving God. I will forgive and remember your sins no more. Ask what you will, and it will be given to you. Seek and you shall find. Knock and it will be opened to you. I have created you in

My fashion. You are becoming more like Me every day. Give—and it shall be given to you. Love—and you will be loved. Forgive—and you will be forgiven. These are My great mysteries: spiritual laws that are not comprehended by natural man."

November 19

Thus saith the Lord;

"I am the way, the truth, and the life. You move and have your being because of Me. I am in control. I hear your prayers and I am answering them. I reassure you again and again. Enjoy your life. Enjoy each day I give you. Be as a child and trust Me. Do not worry. Be happy. You do not have to strive to make things happen. I make them happen."

November 20

Thus saith the Lord;

"All things are possible to him who believes, for if you have faith the size of a mustard seed you can move a mountain. Whatsoever things that you desire when you pray, believe that you receive them before you see them and they shall come to pass. Faith believes without seeing. Your loved ones will come to Me, but not yet. Continue to pray for them. You are My child and I am your Father. Ask what you will and I will give it to you: not by might, not by power, but by My Spirit. All authority has been given to Me. Be full of Me. Live in Me. Breathe in Me. I am life. Your life shall be abundant, overflowing with joy, and lacking nothing. Give—give of yourself, give of your love, give of your talents, and give of all that I freely give to you. You are mine and I love you. Be blessed."

November 21

Thus saith the Lord;

"I cherish these times that we spend together. I need your companionship. I love to commune with My children, the same way that you love to commune with your children. Come to Me often. Come to Me more. I shall never leave you nor forsake you. If you could see everything the way I see them, know everything that I know, you would not be so sad; you would not have a worry or a care; you would not be sick; you would not be depressed; you would not be broken or in financial distress. Give it all to Me! *Learn to live in My freedom!* All things have been given to Me and freely I will give them all to you. You must trust Me and believe that I am all that I say that I am and that I can do all that I say I can do. Have faith, trust, and believe. I am working on your behalf. I love you more than life itself. In fact, I gave My life up for you. Now live! Live your life to its fullest, in My presence, in My perfect love, in My peace, in My joy, in My restoration, in My renewing knowing that you will live eternally with Me in My kingdom."

November 22

Thus saith the Lord;

"You are mine. You belong to Me. There is no returning to your old life. All things are new in Me. I shall take you down the straight and narrow path. You will not veer off. I will be with you all the way. Do not fear. I know the plans that I have for you. They are good. I will pour My thoughts into your thoughts. I will make My plans your plans. You will know My ways. Your faith will increase and all the things that I have done, you can do too, because My power I give to you this day. Use My name, say My name, and say it often because there is power in the name of *Jesus*."

November 23

Thus saith the Lord;

"All that you ask, I can do for you and I will do for you."

November 24

Thus saith the Lord;

"It is My great pleasure to give you great gifts, just as you desire to give to others. You shall not lack; you will not go without. You will not be in need. Your supply shall come, you shall see."

November 25

Thus saith the Lord;

"It is I who gave you life. It is I who saved your soul. It is by My stripes that you are healed. It is I who is by your side. It is I who guides you with My eye. It is I who makes you righteous in My sight. It is you who chose this life with Me. It is by your faith that you were saved. It is by your faith that you are healed. You walk with Me. You follow My path. By coming to Me, you are made righteous. It takes two in union to accomplish My will—you and I. I need you, and you need Me. That is what makes this relationship so special. Thank you."

November 26

Thus saith the Lord;

"Good morning, My child. With each passing day you are growing more like Me. Your knowledge and understanding of Me is increasing. You are beginning to comprehend My power. You believe more and more that I am in control. Your faith in Me is growing. I have proven Myself to you over and over again. My child, continue doing your part and I will continue doing My part. We will be together for all eternity."

November 27

Thus saith the Lord;

"With pain comes growth and wisdom. Much can be accomplished through the pain and suffering endured by a man or woman. Look how much I suffered for all humanity and the accomplishments that came from this endearment. That is why I say that those who can endure until the end will receive the crown of life. Some pain is self-induced and some pain is caused by others. What is important is how you deal with the pain. Seek Me and My help."

November 28

Thus saith the Lord;

"You can run, but you cannot hide. For I, the Lord your God, know all and see all. Do not be ashamed. Repent—for I am a forgiving God. I am just in all My ways. I died that you might live. Do not regret your life, for it was planned by Me. You will accomplish my purposes for you."

November 29

Thus saith the Lord;

"Do not worry or be troubled concerning the lives of those around you. For when they are offered to Me, I truly take care of them. I can be trusted."

November 30

Thus saith the Lord;

"My ways are not your ways. My thoughts are not your thoughts. I see all, know all, and hear all. You must believe and trust that what I am doing in your life is good. I will accomplish My purpose and plan for your life. Give everything to Me. Let My work continue. Do not get in the way. Be as a little child, be humble, let Me lead you, and guide you."

DECEMBER

And it shall come to pass in the last days, says God, That I will pour out of My Spirit on all flesh; Your sons and your daughters shall prophesy, Your young men shall see visions, Your old men shall dream dreams.

Acts 2:17

December 1

Thus saith the Lord;

"You will see many mighty things in the days to come. I will pour out My blessings to you; I will pour out My Spirit to you as mighty rushing waters. You will see prayers answered. Your faith shall increase. Your patience will be rewarded. You will rejoice and be exceedingly glad. This is not the end; it is just the beginning of great things to come."

December 2

Thus saith the Lord;

"Whatsoever things that man has intended for harm, I can turn around for My honor and glory. My blessings are upon you. It is My great pleasure to give you everything that you ask for. Answers are coming. Blessings are coming. Remember, in your hour of receiving your blessings, you must pass some on to others. Then more will come. Then give more. Just as it delights you to give to others, it also delights Me to give to those that ask. Ask and it shall be given. Knock and I will open the door. See My beauty in the world all around you. Look for the good in all. I love everyone and you must too. Sing a song. Rejoice and be exceedingly glad, for this is the day that I have made."

December 3

Thus saith the Lord;

"I feel your pain, My precious child. I have come to give you life, a more abundant life. I will open doors for you that you never thought would open. I will lead you to a land flowing with milk and honey. I am pouring out My Spirit to you—breathe in—breathe in My Spirit, for a renewing, a life-changing renewal that can only come from Me. Remember, you have Me in your life. My strength I give to you, My peace I give to you. I know the hearts of men. I will send visions to them and dreams. I will continue to knock until they let Me in.

I long for the lost and I will bring them back to Me. This is My promise. Can you hold on to this secret promise of mine? No matter what happens? No matter how long it takes?"

December 4

Thus saith the Lord;

"Not by might, not by power, but by My Spirit; I can touch and change the hearts of men, women, and children. My grace is sufficient for you. All that you have asked, I will do. Trust in Me. I do not necessarily work in the way you think I should. Your ways are not My ways. Your thoughts are not My thoughts. Your time is not My time. Be patient and trust Me, My child. For, I am the All Knowing, All Mighty God. If you could only know all the plans I have for you, you would not worry anymore. It is too much for you to know all that I have in store for your life. I only reveal in part; what is necessary for you right now. Live one day at a time. Forget the past. Forget your failures. Live only for Me and only for this day. You cannot change the plans that I have for you. You can only delay them. Change will come. Change is good. I do not change, for I am the same yesterday, today, and forever."

December 5

Thus saith the Lord;

"What God hath joined together let no man break apart. As long as there is a will there is a way. Have faith and be of a good cheer. I am the Healer and the Maker of the universe. Many I have called, but few have answered."

December 6

Thus saith the Lord;

"My hand is upon you. Do you not know that even judges hearken unto Me? If I am for you, who can be against you? Where I lead, you will follow. What I say, you will say. You know My voice and you will not be led astray. You are My beloved child in whom I am well pleased. Continue in Me and I will continue in you. Ask what you will, and I will do it for you, for I am a rewarder of those who diligently seek Me. I am compassionate to the fatherless, the husbandless, the widow, and the single parent. My mercies are endless. My grace is sufficient. My glory is magnificent. So live! Live without fear. Live without worry. Lift your cares and concerns to Me, and I will fulfill your every desire. Be blessed, My child. Be blessed."

December 7

Thus saith the Lord;

"Be patient My child. When the time is right you will know; for now, be still and know that I am God."

December 8

Thus saith the Lord;

"Things are not as bad as they may seem. For you only see in part—what is here and now. I see the whole picture. I know the plans I have for you: your future, tomorrow, and eternity. I have not abandoned you. Although the road may seem rough and weary, I go before you to light the way. Continue to walk My way. Remember growing pains are not always pleasant. Do you want Me to continue working in your life, or would you have Me stop? I love you and I will never give you more than what you can handle. Rejoice! I see progress in your life and in My plans for you. Lift your chin up, for the victory is yours; you will not be beaten down, trod under, or cast down. I am in you, I am your strength, and I am working for you. Be blessed."

December 9

Thus saith the Lord;

"My eyes are on you and I hear all that you have to say. I love when you commune with Me. It brings Me great joy. I love your faithfulness. You have a sweet spirit. It moves Me. Have a wonderful, blessed day. Be full of My joy. Let's spend the day together and be lifted up by each other. Pray for those who cross your path today. I will be with you. Feel My presence. My anointing is upon you. Whatsoever things you are compelled to do—do in My name. I send you to a lost and dying world. Many need My touch. Touch many lives for My kingdom's sake."

December 10

Thus saith the Lord;

"By My mighty hand, I will bring down the walls that hold you back. I will break the chains that have you bound. I will deliver you from this present evil; not by might, not by power, but by My Spirit saith the Lord. Be diligent, stay in My Word, and stay close to Me. Pray without ceasing; believe the things that I tell you; plant your feet on My Words, for it is a rock that keeps you from falling. Fear not: for everything that I ask you to do, I have already gone before you and prepared your way. The work would almost be done, except I need the faith-filled believer to put My desire and My Words into action. I know your heart and it belongs to Me. Your love for Me is strong and your works do not go unnoticed, nor your prayers unanswered. I love you."

December 11

Thus saith the Lord;

"My hand is upon you and all that you do. You will be blessed when you come in and blessed when you go out. Again, I say to you, do not fret what tomorrow may hold because it is not here yet. I give you only what you need for today. My preparations are under way, and when it is time they will be revealed to you. Cherish every moment of each new day, for today will never come again. Again, I say to you, do not be sad! I know the beginning until the end. I have a perfect plan for you and you cannot change these plans. I will lead you where you need to go. I will provide for your every need. Live like a child: no worries, no cares, and have fun. Choose to live a life of joy. My joy I have given to you."

December 12

Thus saith the Lord;

"This day, nothing will come your way that you cannot handle, for I am with you. My power I give to you: the power of life and death. There is power in the tongue; it is sharper than any two-edged sword. The tongue has power to heal, power to give life, and power to kill. Be careful what you say and what you speak to others. Do not speak out of anger, for you can tear down all that I have been building up. Therefore, be slow to speak. Speak those things that I give you to speak. Encourage one another. Be a servant, just as I was sent to serve. Bring peace wherever you go. When you do not feel peace it is because I am not present. Seek Me and My kingdom, and all things will be added to you."

December 13

Thus saith the Lord;

"Blessings, Honor, and joy are coming. My glory will shine. It will shine through your turmoil. It will shine through your circumstances. Do not fret. Do not feel sorry for yourself, for there are so many others less fortunate than you. Many have greater problems than you. Pray for others. Lift the burdens of other people, and it will also help lighten your load. Try to bless someone else's day and you will be blessed too."

December 14

Thus saith the Lord;

"Delight thyself also in the Lord and He will give thee the desires of thine heart. Trust in Him with your whole heart and lean not to your own understanding. Acknowledge Him in all your ways and He will direct your path. Bless the Lord all you inhabitants of the earth. Bless His Holy name. All good and perfect gifts come from the Father above whose name is worthy to be praised, whose eye is continually upon you, and His Spirit dwells inside of you. He does not sleep and is ever waiting to spend time with you. Seek Him and His kingdom and all things will be added to you."

December 15

Thus saith the Lord;

"My kingdom will come. My kingdom will come and you will be a part of it. Preparations are being made continuously. I am preparing a special place for you and your loved ones to spend in eternity with Me. Rejoice and be exceedingly glad. There will be no more sorrow, no more sickness or disease, no more pain and suffering. The glory of the Lord will be there—*in all His glory*. He will be magnificent and lifted up. His name will be exalted continuously. He will be praised and worshipped non-stop. The singing there will be glorious, and we will see God on His throne. *Glory! Glory! Glory! Our God is mighty*. Let us worship Him every day in preparation of His glorious return, until we can be there with Him. HALLELUJAH!"

December 16

Thus saith the Lord;

"I love you and you are special to Me. You cannot change people. That is My work to accomplish. You can only help guide and point the way. My work begins on the inside and is not always visible.

I will accomplish all that I have said I will do. Do not let vain imaginations rule your mind. Cast them down. It is I who will mold and make you into My image. All that I do is good. Rejoice and be exceedingly glad."

December 17

Thus saith the Lord;

"I am the potter and you are the clay. I am making and molding you into My image. I am pouring My desires into your heart and mind. You will begin to see others the way I see them. You will desire the things that I desire. I will take you into a deeper walk with Me. You feel My presence. You feel My peace. You feel My love. You will feel My longing desire to see all men saved. I will be your closest friend, and the more you get to know me, the more that you will become like me. Nothing is too hard for Me, and nothing is impossible for Me. You shall see many mighty things in the days to come. I AM GOD."

December 18

Thus saith the Lord;

"My eyes are upon you and all that you do. Nothing goes unnoticed. No, not even the smallest things. I test the hearts. I know the minds. Even your thoughts are known by Me. Give Me your heart, give Me your mind, give Me your mouth, your hands, your feet, your will, and your desires. Give Me everything, so I can use you the way that I want to use you. Surrender it all. Say, 'Lord I surrender all to you, my Lord *Jesus*.' Now I am free to have My way with you, and power will freely flow so My kingdom will come like heaven on earth. Then we can become as one. My mouth can become your mouth; My hands can become your hands; My will can become your will; My heart can become your heart. Truly, My work can be done through you, for you and for others. Magnify His Holy name. You truly will be just like Me."

December 19

Thus saith the Lord;

"I am coming. I am coming again to gather those who belong to Me, to take with Me, to be with Me for all eternity. What a glorious day that will be. Know that you are chosen. Know that you belong to Me and that you cannot be taken away from Me. I will keep you under the shadow of My wings and protect you."

December 20

Thus saith the Lord;

"My blessings are bountiful and never ending. Again I say to you that you shall see many mighty things in the days to come. My hand is upon you and all that you do."

December 21

Thus saith the Lord;

"Have no fear what tomorrow may bring, for I supply all that you need for today."

December 22

Thus saith the Lord;

"Purify and cleanse yourself because the day is coming when judgment shall fall."

December 23

Thus saith the Lord;

"I came into the world for you, a dying people that you might live. I made the way: the path to a new and better life that you might escape the snares of the devil. It is a path, long and straight, for all to follow. I have made the way easy, even for the young, to know and come to me. All are called, but few are chosen. It is a choice and not all will choose Me and My ways. The plan is simple, but the steps are not always easy. To those who endure until the end, the reward will be spectacular. I will be there with you all the way, helping, encouraging, loving, and pointing the way. My grace is sufficient. My mercies are new every day. Seek Me in secret, and I will reward you openly. Pray without ceasing. Trust Me and your joy will be full. I did all this, and much more will I do because I love you. Be blessed, My precious child, be blessed."

December 24

Thus saith the Lord;

"I am the Lord your God. I go before you this day. Everything that comes to you has already been filtered through my hands first. For all things are held in My mighty hands. Nothing can touch you without My permission first, as long as you are walking with Me, in My Spirit, in My presence, in My will, and close to Me. I uphold you with My hand. Your footsteps are ordered by Me. My eye is guiding you. My protection is upon you. My peace I give to you. You are a delight, and I love to spend time together. Continue with Me this day, and I will reveal many things to you. Lift souls to Me, lift burdens to Me. Give Me your all, and I will give you rest. Do not worry; great things are about to come, and you will be exceedingly glad. Begin to rejoice. Again, I say rejoice, and this will release abundant blessings in your life."

December 25

Thus saith the Lord;

"Whatsoever things you desire when you pray, believe that you receive them and you will have them, for faith does believe even when it cannot be seen. It is My great privilege to give you all things: the things that you need, spiritual gifts, and the things that you desire. All belongs to Me and I have power over everything. I speak and it is done. There is power in your words too. Speak good things. Build up others, and so let your light shine. You can be a blessing or a curse. There is power in the tongue. If someone curses you, rebuke it, and command it to return to where it came. No harm shall come to you."

December 26

Thus saith the Lord;

"My hand is mighty to save. I formed the earth and all that is within it in six days. I can speak a Word, and it is done. Where is your faith? How many times must I tell you? You will see many mighty things come to pass. You will see every prayer answered. It will be in My time, when the time is right. You must be obedient, and do the things that I have told you to do. Use My strength when you have none. Use My power because I give it to you. Use My Name because it is the Name above all Names containing All Authority, which I have given to you. Believe Me. Trust Me. I will reveal the perfect plan to you in full. Now, you can only see in part. I love you and I care for you. *Be confident!* **Know that I am God!**"

December 27

Thus saith the Lord;

"A happy heart is a prayerful heart. A prayerful heart is a praising heart. Praise sets My power into motion. Praise sends the enemy fleeing. Praise increases faith. Praise is what My angels do, so your praise puts you in the same stature as My angels. It satisfies Me. It brings Me much pleasure. It draws Me closer to you. It brings Me honor. It brings Me glory. I am your God and you are My child, in whom I am well pleased. I find pleasure in you. My blessings I give to you."

December 28

Thus saith the Lord;

"No man has ever seen God in all His glory. The day is coming when every knee shall bow and every tongue will confess that He is Lord, and you will see Him face to face in all His glory. You shall be partakers in His kingdom and you will reign with Him forevermore. Everything will be revealed. Nothing will be hidden and you will spend eternity in His presence. His glory will shine."

December 29

Thus saith the Lord;

"I need obedient people to do the things that I ask of them no matter how small or silly they may sound. I need strong hands and willing minds to serve Me and do the things that I ask, for you are My feet and My hands. I will use your mouth to speak to others. I need you. I need your help. You are more valuable to Me than rubies or gold. Together, you and I—the work place could be changed—the city you live in could be changed—the state you live in could be changed—the country you live in could be changed. In fact, the whole world can be changed. Pray! Pray without ceasing. Pray for the whole world. Release My Spirit. Release My power and let Me do the rest. Well done, faithful servant."

December 30

Thus saith the Lord;

"My ways are not your ways. My thoughts are not your thoughts. That is why it is important to ask for My guidance and My wisdom. I am ever changing your thoughts and minds to conform to mine. It is important to acknowledge Me in all your ways, so I can direct your paths. I keep you from evil. I keep you from stumbling. When you are at peace, it is because you are in My will. Continue to go forward with no fear, because I go before you. I am preparing the way to a brighter and more fulfilling future. Put your trust in

Me. Love Me and commune with Me. These are the things that I need. Yes, I need you just like you need Me. This day you will be blessed."

December 31

Thus saith the Lord;

"Get Ready! Again, I say: Get Ready! Get your house in order, and do the things you ought to do to get prepared. Pray for My will to be done in your life and the lives of those around you. Forgive everyone that ought to be forgiven. Hold no grudges. Let My love shine through you. The hour is coming that no man knows, not even Me. Only the Father knows. The son of God will return to take what belongs to Him. I say to you: pray—that you will be ready."

Thus saith the Lord;

"The time is now. He whom you seek is coming!"

God moves people in and out of our lives for specific purposes. Sometimes it is for our benefit and sometimes it is for the benefit of others. It is all for His specific purpose and plan in our life. God birthed the thought of this book in my mind and put the desire in my heart to allow Him to use me for His specific purpose of speaking to His people. To encourage, and uplift, to bless and increase the faith of those who believe in Him. There have been several different people, at one time or another, sent across my path, to help fulfill the plans for this book. Some of whom were my prayer partners. I want to thank Peg and Aunt Sue for their prayer support. I want to thank June for her dedication, prayer support, and editorial skills donated to this book. I want to thank John for his picture on the front cover. I want to thank Phil and Dianne for their help. I also want to thank my loving daughters, Jennifer and Joannie, my mother, and my husband, Joseph, and my beautiful grandchildren, for their support and understanding through my trying times. (Even though they did not know what I had to go through to receive God's Word.) I had to endure much sadness, pain, depression, suffering and loneliness to draw closer to God to receive these Words from the Lord, for His lost and dying world, in which case, I have been blessed. May you be blessed by the Words of the Lord, our God, creator and maker of the universe from whom all blessings flow.

Tamara Dreier, (instrument of God)